# OUTSTANDING STORIES
## by General Authorities

# OUTSTANDING STORIES
## by General Authorities

Compiled by Leon R. Hartshorn

Published by
Deseret Book Company
Salt Lake City, Utah
1978

ISBN number 0-87747-369-2
Library of Congress No. 73-136-241


Copyright 1970
by
Deseret Book Company

# Table of Contents

*Page*

## Elder Hugh B. Brown

Picture ------------------------------------------------ x
Biographical Sketch----------------------------------- 1
    "Father, Are You There?" --------------------- 3
    "I Only Touched Ground Once" ---------------- 4
    "Will You Give Me My Life" ------------------ 8
    "The Identification of Jock Anderson" ------------ 10
    "Thank You, God" --------------------------- 12
    "I Cannot Buy That with Money" --------------- 16
    "The Gardener and the Currant Bush" ------------ 19

## Bishop Victor L. Brown

Picture ------------------------------------------------ 22
Biographical Sketch----------------------------------- 23
    "Bobby Polacio"----------------------------- 25
    "Michael and Bill" --------------------------- 27

## President Paul H. Dunn

Picture ------------------------------------------------ 32
Biographical Sketch----------------------------------- 33
    "Call from the Prophet" ---------------------- 35
    "A Missionary Inquires"---------------------- 39
    "A Tribute to the Church"--------------------- 41
    "A New Ball Glove" -------------------------- 43
    "I Had Really Earned My Letter" --------------- 45
    "You Don't Look Like What You Are Supposed to Be" -- 48
    "Lou Brisse" ------------------------------- 50
    "I Might Get HIM as a Son-in-law" ------------- 53
    "Yes, Sir" --------------------------------- 54
    "Give Me a New Thought" -------------------- 57
    "The New Testament Really Works" ------------- 59
    "He is a Priesthood Man" --------------------- 63
    "Love, Your Home Teacher"-------------------- 64
    "Death in a Foxhole" ------------------------- 68
    "Staff Sergeant Isso" ------------------------- 69
    "Six Feet Four Inches Tall and a Spirit to Match" ----- 72

## Elder Alvin R. Dyer

| | | Page |
|---|---|---|
| Picture | | 78 |
| Biographical Sketch | | 79 |
| "Would You Like to Know More?" | | 83 |
| "Dad Wants You to Come Back" | | 84 |
| "The Font Is Filled" | | 85 |
| "The Mayor of Reykjavik" | | 86 |
| "Elder Kahne" | | 90 |
| "Why These Are Our Teachings!" | | 92 |

## Elder Marion D. Hanks

| | | |
|---|---|---|
| Picture | | 94 |
| Biographical Sketch | | 95 |
| "Look, You Can't Do This to Me" | | 97 |
| "Ah, Let Him Go, He Is Just One Kid!" | | 99 |
| "The Courage of Sergeant 'Red' Irwin" | | 102 |
| "A Sacred Experience" | | 103 |
| "Kneel Down, Son" | | 105 |
| "Boy, We Really Have A Swell Bathroom, Haven't We" | | 107 |
| "Say, Hanks, Do You Believe in Jesus Christ?" | | 108 |
| "I Won't Stand Between You and God" | | 110 |
| "Gerry" | | 111 |
| "Happiest Birthday" | | 113 |
| "I'm Too Busy Building Fires" | | 114 |
| "Daddy, I Wish You Could Be with Me" | | 115 |
| "To Whoever Finds This" | | 117 |
| "Wait a Minute" | | 117 |
| "Donna" | | 120 |
| "Lord, Help Me Know" | | 124 |
| "Could We Wait Until Monday?" | | 126 |

## Elder Gordon B. Hinckley

| | | |
|---|---|---|
| Picture | | 128 |
| Biographical Sketch | | 129 |
| "Fear of Ridicule" | | 131 |
| "He Was Talking About My Boy" | | 132 |
| "He Didn't Have Enough Sense to Wear Shoes" | | 134 |
| "A 1916 Model T Ford" | | 135 |
| "My Mission Is a Failure" | | 135 |
| "Will He Come Back?" | | 136 |
| "Can I Get a Copy of That Book?" | | 139 |

## Elder Howard W. Hunter

| | | |
|---|---|---|
| Picture | | 140 |
| Biographical Sketch | | 141 |
| "It All Started from a Prayer That Night" | | 143 |

## Elder John Longden         *Page*

Picture ------------------------------------------- 148
Biographical Sketch------------------------------- 149
    "I Tried to Speak English and I Could Not" --------- 151
    "Clarence Romeral, a Mormon Boy"--------------- 152
    "Going to New Zealand" --------------------- 154

## Elder LeGrand Richards

Picture ------------------------------------------- 156
Biographical Sketch------------------------------- 157
    "Thirty-five Million Years from Today"------------ 159
    "I Laid My Bible on the Table" ---------------- 160
    "A Little for Good Measure" ------------------ 161
    "The Lord's Blueprint" --------------------- 162
    "I Am Afraid to Go Home" ------------------ 164
    "A Chance to Get Even" -------------------- 165
    "It Is Now 165 Years" --------------------- 167
    "You Can't Get Away from Love Like That" --------- 168
    "Our Hearts Have Been Comforted"-------------- 169

## Bishop Robert L. Simpson

Picture ------------------------------------------- 172
Biographical Sketch------------------------------- 173
    "The Entire Maori Battalion" ------------------ 175
    "Chant of the Old Maoris"------------------- 178
    "The Wyoming Cowboy" -------------------- 179
    "From the Mission Office" ------------------- 181
    "Last Testimonies" ----------------------- 182

## Elder Alma Sonne

Picture ------------------------------------------- 184
Biographical Sketch------------------------------- 185
    "Bishop, Let's Ride to the Top of the Mountain" ------ 187
    "We Love to Sing" ----------------------- 191

## President Nathan Eldon Tanner

Picture ------------------------------------------- 196
Biographical Sketch------------------------------- 197
    "Have a Good Time" ---------------------- 199
    "You and the Rest of the World"---------------- 200
    "I Am Going to Report to the Lord Tonight"--------- 202
    "The Value of a Good Home"------------------ 203
    "I Can't Think of a Good Reason Why I Should" ------ 204
    "He Had Real Courage" -------------------- 205
    "That Is What I Am Saying to You Today, Mr.
        Armstrong" ------------------------- 207
    "Preparing for a Mission"------------------- 209
    "Why Can't You Pray Where You Are?" ----------- 210

*Page*

"Safely in West Berlin" --------------------- 211
"He Was Prepared to Go the Extra Mile" ---------- 212
"I Thought I Could Depend on You" ------------- 213

## President A. Theodore Tuttle

Picture ------------------------------------ 214
Biographical Sketch--------------------------- 215
"Thank You" ----------------------------- 217
"Every Time I Open the Closet" ---------------- 218
"He Was Obviously from the Farm"-------------- 219
"A Young Boy's Answer" --------------------- 220
"We Made a Covenant" --------------------- 221
"Let It Fly Clear up to the Sky" ---------------- 222

## President S. Dilworth Young

Picture ------------------------------------ 224
Biographical Sketch--------------------------- 225
"An Accounting" ------------------------- 227
"I'm Going to Give You a Warning Ticket" --------- 228
"If It Is Told About You"--------------------- 230

# Biographical Sketch

## ELDER HUGH B. BROWN

A former army officer, practicing attorney, college professor and oil company executive, Elder Hugh B. Brown was called to be a member of the Council of Twelve Apostles on April 6, 1958, after he had served as an Assistant to the Council since 1953. He was named a member of the First Presidency on June 22, 1961 and served as First Counselor to President David O. McKay until the President's death on January 18, 1970, at which time Elder Brown resumed his position in the Quorum of the Twelve.

He was born in Salt Lake City, Utah, October 24, 1883, second son and fifth of fourteen children of Homer Manley and Lydia J. B. Brown. The family moved to Canada fifteen years later and much of Elder Brown's life has been centered there. He married Zina Young Card, daughter of Charles O. Card (founder of Cardston, Alta., Canada) and grand-daughter of Brigham Young, June 17, 1908, in the Salt Lake Temple. They have six daughters and a son living. Another son, Hugh Card Brown, was killed in World War II.

Elder Brown first practiced law in Canada and later in the United States. During World War I, he served overseas in the

Canadian Army, attaining the rank of major. He was professor of religion and coordinator of veterans affairs at Brigham Young University from 1946 to 1950. And at the time of his call to be one of the Church's General Authorities, Elder Brown was president and manager of the Richland Oil Development Company of Canada, Ltd.

His present responsibility has been preceded by years of Church service. He was a missionary in Great Britain, 1904-6, and subsequently has been a bishop's counselor, Alberta (Canada) Stake high councilman, Lethbridge (Canada) stake president; Granite (Salt Lake City) counselor and stake president; and twice (1937-40 and 1944-46) British Mission president. During World War II, he was coordinator of LDS servicemen's activities.

# HUGH B. BROWN

*"Father, Are You There?"*

**I** think one of the first things that
every young person should do is attempt to get acquainted with
God. I mean that in a very literal sense. I mean it in the sense
that we are able to go to him and obtain the kind of help that
we need. I remember when I was quite a lad (and that's remem-
bering a long way back)—I remember my mother said to me
when I went to go on my mission in 1904 (and that's before
some of you were born)—she said, "My boy, you are going a
long ways away from me now. Do you remember," she said,
"that when you were a little lad you used to have bad dreams
and get frightened? Your bedroom was just off mine, and frequently you would cry out in the night and say, 'Mother, are
you there?' And I would answer 'Yes, my boy, I'm here—
everything is all right. Turn over and go to sleep.' You always
did. Knowing that I was there gave you courage.

"Now," she said, "you will be about 6,000 miles away,
and though you may cry out for me I cannot answer you."
She added this: "There is one who can, and if you call to him,
He'll hear you when you call. He will respond to your appeal.
You just say, 'Father, are you there?' and there will come into

3

your heart the comfort and solace such as you knew as a boy when I answered you."

I want to say to you young people that many times since then in many and varying conditions I have cried out, "Father, are you there?" I made that plea when in the mission field we were mobbed almost every night, driven from place to place. We were beaten, expelled from cities, our lives threatened. Every time before I went out to those meetings I would say, "Father, are you there?" And though I didn't hear a voice and I didn't see his person, I want to tell you young people he replied to me with the comfort and assurance and testimony of his presence. It made me unafraid; and with that presence, I am grateful to say, we did not suffer much.

---

(*BYU Stakes Fireside Address,* "Father, Are You There?" October 8, 1967 [Provo, Utah: Brigham Young University Press], pp. 5-6.)

HUGH B. BROWN

---

## *"I Only Touched Ground Once"*

I would like to call your attention to what happens to a man in this church when he is converted to the truth. I hope you are all converts. I was in a meeting not long ago and I asked how many were converts. Probably fifty per cent raised their hands. I said, "I advise the rest of you to get converted." You need to be converts. I would like to say this in passing, that in the years that have passed, and they are many, I have continued to be a convert to The Church of Jesus Christ of Latter-day Saints; and for that I thank God. He has been good to me in that he has headed me off when I would have gone my own way. He has known better than I do what was good for me, and he has been willing and gracious to make provision for the things that he could see and I couldn't would happen to me, unless he took a part; and he took it. For this I am extremely grateful.

I said I have had contact with him. In 1904 I went to England on a mission. President Grant sent me down to Norwich. When I got into Norwich the president of the district sent me down to Cambridge. He said, "I want you to go with Elder Downs (he was a man 45 years old and I was 21). Elder Downs will leave the morning after you get there for France, because his mission is completed. There is not another Latter-day Saint within 120 miles of Cambridge, so you will be alone." He said, "You might be interested to know, Brother Brown, that the last Mormon elder that was in Cambridge was driven out by a mob at the point of a gun and was told the next Mormon elder that stepped inside the city limits would be shot on sight." He said, "I thought you would be glad to know that."

I wasn't glad to know it, but I thought it was well that I did know it.

We went to Cambridge. There were great signs all over the city—they had heard we were coming. They had signs indicating their antipathy. That was their method of welcoming us. One big sign at the railway station was of a large man with a long beard, with a woman lying at his feet with her head on a block. Underneath it said, "Will you go into polygamy or won't you?" That was the reception we received.

Elder Downs left the next morning after telling me how to prepare my tracts, and I went out on Friday morning and tracted all morning without any response except a slammed door in my face. I tracted all afternoon with the same response, and I came home pretty well discouraged. But I decided to tract Saturday morning, although it wasn't required. I went out and tracted all morning and got the same results. I came home dejected and downhearted, and I thought I ought to go home. I thought the Lord had made a mistake in sending me to Cambridge.

I was sitting by that little alleged fire they have in England,

5

with a big granddaddy clock at the side of the so-called fire. I was feeling sorry for myself, and I heard a knock at the front door. The lady of the house answered the door. I heard a voice say, "Is there an Elder Brown lives here?" I thought, "Oh, oh, here it is!"

She said, "Why, yes, he's in the front room. Come in, please."

He came in and said, "Are you Elder Brown?"

I was not surprised that he was surprised. I said, "Yes, sir."

He said, "Did you leave this tract at my door?"

Well, my name and address were on it. Though I was attempting at that time to get ready to practice law, I didn't know how to answer it. I said, "Yes, sir, I did."

He said, "Last Sunday there were seventeen of us heads of families left the Church of England. We went to my home where I have a rather large room. Each of us has a large family, and we filled the large room with men, women and children. We decided that we would pray all through the week that the Lord would send us a new pastor. When I came home tonight I was discouraged; I thought our prayer had not been answered. But when I found this tract under my door, I knew the Lord had answered our prayer. Will you come tomorrow night and be our new pastor?"

Now, I hadn't been in the mission field three days. I didn't know anything about missionary work, and he wanted me to be their pastor. But I was reckless enough to say, "Yes, I'll come." And I repented from then till tne time of the meeting.

He left, and took my appetite with him! I called in the lady of the house and told her I didn't want any tea. I went up to my room and prepared for bed. I knelt at my bed. My young brothers and sisters, for the first time in my life I talked with God. I told him of my predicament. I pleaded for his help. I asked him to guide me. I pleaded that he would take it off my hands. I got up and went to bed and couldn't sleep and got out and prayed again, and kept that up all night—but I really talked with God.

The next morning I told the landlady I didn't want any breakfast, and I went up on the campus in Cambridge and walked all morning. I came in at noon and told her I didn't want any lunch. Then I walked all afternoon. I had a short-circuited mind—all that I could think of was that I have got to go down there tonight and be a pastor.

I came back to my room at 6:00 and I sat there meditating, worrying, wondering. (Let me in parenthesis tell you that since that time I have had the experience of sitting beside a man who was condemned to die the next morning. As I sat and watched his emotions I was reminded of how I felt that night. I think I felt just as bad as he did.) The execution time was drawing near. Finally it came to the point where the clock said 6:45. I got up and put on my long Prince Albert coat, my stiff hat which I had acquired in Norwich, took my walking cane (which we always carried in those days), my kid gloves, put a Bible under my arm, and dragged myself down to that building, literally. I just made one track all the way.

Just as I got to the gate the man came out, the man I had seen the night before. He bowed very politely and said, "Come in, Reverend, sir." I had never been called that before. I went in and saw the room filled with people, and they all stood up to honor their new pastor, and that scared me to death.

Then I had come to the point where I began to think what I had to do, and I realized I had to say something about singing. I suggested that we sing "O My Father." I was met with a blank stare. We sang it—it was a terrible cowboy solo. Then I thought, if I could get these people to turn around and kneel by their chairs, they wouldn't be looking at me while I prayed. I asked them if they would and they responded readily. They all knelt down, and I knelt down, and for the second time in my life I talked with God. All fear left me. I didn't worry any more. I was turning it over to him.

I said to him, among other things, "Father in Heaven, these folks have left the Church of England. They have come here tonight to hear the truth. You know that I am not prepared to give them what they want, but Thou art, O God, the one that can; and if I can be an instrument through whom You speak, very well, but please take over."

When we arose most of them were weeping, as was I.

Wisely I dispensed with the second hymn, and I started to talk. I talked forty-five minutes. I don't know what I said. I didn't talk—God spoke through me, as subsequent events proved. And he spoke so powerfully to that group that at the close of that meeting they came and put their arms around me, held my hands. They said, "This is what we have been waiting for. Thank God you came."

I told you I dragged myself down to that meeting. On my way back home that night I only touched ground once, I was so elated that God had taken off my hands an insuperable task for man.

Within three months every man, woman and child in that audience was baptized a member of the Church. I didn't baptize them because I was transferred. But they all joined the Church and most of them came to Utah and Idaho. I have seen some of them in recent years. They are elderly people now, but they say they never have attended such a meeting, a meeting where God spoke to them.

(*BYU Stakes Fireside Address*, "Father, Are You There?" October 8, 1967, pp. 12-15.)

# HUGH B. BROWN

## *"Will You Give Me My Life"*

As has been mentioned, I was at one time an army officer. As such, I became accustomed to having men stand at attention and salute me and call me "sir," and frankly, I liked it.

Often men came and asked for favors—perhaps a furlough or a leave or something that they thought I could grant—because they knew that I was an officer of the King and that I had the right to speak in his name. And so as they came I handed the "blessings" down to them, and I became more haughty and self-important with each event.

One day a messenger came to my hotel just off Piccadilly Circus. He said, "You are wanted immediately in the hospital."

I thought, "Well, here is another boy that wants something. I will go down and see what is wanted."

I called a taxi and went to the hospital.

When I arrived the doctors stood at attention and saluted, and that fed my ego. The nurses treated me with great respect, and that pleased me even more.

They directed me to a little room, and as I pushed open the door, I saw an emaciated young man lying on a cot. I recognized him as a former Sunday School student of mine in Cardston, Canada.

When he greeted me, he did not use my rank in his salutation, but simply said, "Brother Brown, I sent for you to ask if you would use your authority in my behalf." (I thought, "Well, this is what I expected. What does he want?")

"Brother Brown," he said, "you know I have a widowed mother; I am her only son. The doctors say I cannot live; will you give me my life?"

I thought, "My goodness, the King of England can't give him his life. To what is he referring?"

Then he startled me with a request: "Will you administer to me!"

At that moment, my young friends, my uniform, with the insignia on it, seemed to melt away, and I stood before that young man in a uniform, which was next to my skin, if I had not had some authority given to me. I stood there thinking of that authority, and I was humbled but inspired.

I went over to his cot and knelt beside him. I put my hands on his head and said, "In the name of Jesus Christ and by the authority of the holy priesthood, I bless you and promise you that you will get well and return to your mother." God honored that promise.

I went into that hospital a proud British officer, and I came out a humble Mormon elder. Ever since then I have earnestly tried to remember that there is a power and authority given to man, not from the king or the president, but from the King of kings. And if we live properly and do not forget that we have been so endowed, we may exercise that authority in behalf of those who need our ministration.

That divine spark which is in man persists, even though we smother it or try to kill it.

---

(*BYU Speeches of the Year*, "Be What You Will To Be," February 14, 1967, pp. 8-9.)

---

# HUGH B. BROWN

## *"The Identification of Jock Anderson"*

I am thinking in terms, at the moment, of an experience I had when returning from the First World War. I always hesitate to tell these experiences of the First World War because they definitely date me as approaching middle life. I was there in 1915 to 1918 and saw many things and experienced some things, but I'm thinking of a certain man who was known to us in the regiment as the "unsentimental cuss." He was a man apparently without any feeling, a man who was not touched by the things that affect most of us at times, a man who could stand by his comrades and see them shot down and never bat an eye. He was the kind of fellow that most of us—as we noted his actions and his attitudes, heard his coarse language, and saw him in debauchery at times—most of us became for the moment like the Pharisees of old and said in our hearts, though we didn't have the courage to say it out loud, "I thank thee, God, that I'm not like that." I felt that way. And I was a Pharisee.

We got over to France finally. And there it became the duty of the officers to read the incoming and outgoing mail. A very interesting assignment, incidentally. You learn a lot of things that way. This man was on duty reading the mail. He was a captain. He read a letter from a woman in Ontario, Canada, Mrs. Jock Anderson. She had written to her husband. It was impressed on my memory because of what happened subsequently. She said among other things, "My darling, Jock. I'm so happy to have you where you are. We're all so proud of what you're doing. The ten little bairns are coming along all right. I had to wean the baby because I have to work to help with the separation allowance the government gives us. But we're all right, Jock, and if God should see fit to take your life, we'll carry on. But, oh Jock, darling, won't you plead with God with me that he will never allow us to receive word that you are missing?" She said, "Poor Mrs. Johnson next door received that word two months ago, and she's almost frantic. She'd much rather have heard he was dead. Pray God with me Jock, that I may never get word you are missing."

That was the letter this "unsentimental cuss" read. And that night there appeared before him a sergeant and six men. They were to go out into no-man's land on a very dangerous mission. The sergeant read the roll, and the men responded to their names, and one of them was Jock Anderson. They went out, and in the early morning three of them came back with the sergeant. And again he called the roll. And they answered. But Jock Anderson was not among them. This unsentimental man—of whom I said I thank God that I'm not like him—said, "Sergeant, do you know where Jock Anderson fell?"

"Yes, sir. He was on an elevated piece of land covered by a German machine gun."

"Would it be possible, Sergeant, for a man to go out and get his identification disc?" You remember that each soldier had a disc around his neck, and there was a definite rule that unless you could produce his identification disc or his body, you could not report him dead no matter how many men saw him fall. And so the captain said, "Could you get his disc from where he is?"

The sergeant said, "No sir, it would be absolute suicide, but if you say so, I'll try."

The captain said, "No, I didn't mean that. I just wanted to know."

And that night the captain was missing. No one knew where he had gone. And the next morning there came a large envelope, a military envelope, and upon opening it we read, "Dear Major, I am enclosing herewith the identification disc of Jock Anderson. Will you please send word to Mrs. Anderson that God heard her prayer? Her husband is not missing. He's dead." And then he added, as though it didn't amount to anything, "As for me, I'm off to Blighty in the morning. The doctor says it's an amputation case and may prove fatal. Cheerio."

And that was the man who had the intestinal fortitude to crawl out at night alone up to a dead man's body and get a disc from his neck in order that his wife could have the poor satisfaction of learning that her husband was not missing. Many times since then I have felt to say in my heart, "Help me, oh God, never to judge another man. However he may appear, there is something in him better than I.

---

("The Measure of a Man," An address to Seminary and Institute Personnel, July 14, 1966.)

---

### HUGH B. BROWN

---

## *"Thank You, God"*

While I was acting as servicemen's coordinator, I was in London, England. I sent the following telegram to the senior chaplain of a large camp near Liverpool: "I'll be in your camp tomorrow morning at 10:00. Kindly notify all Mormon boys in your camp that we'll hold a meeting."

When I arrived the next morning I met seventy-five young

men, all in uniform. They were delighted to see me, although I knew none of them. They were glad to see someone from home.

There stepped out from the crowd a man who, after shaking hands, said, "I'm the one to whom you sent your telegram. I'm the chaplain of this camp. I didn't get your telegram until this morning (that is, Sunday morning). Upon receipt of it, I made an inquiry—a careful inquiry. I found there were seventy-six Mormon boys in this camp. Seventy-five of them are here, one is in the hospital."

He said, "I wish you'd tell me, Mr. Brown, how you do it. I have six hundred men in my church in this camp, and if I gave them six months notice they couldn't meet that record. Tell me how you do it."

"Well," I said, "if you come into our meeting we'll show you how we do it." And so he accompanied me into the quonset hut, and before us sat these seventy-five young men. I had the minister sit next to me.

I said, "How many of you fellows have been on missions?" Fully fifty percent of them raised their hands. I pointed to six of them and said, "Come here and administer the sacrament." I pointed to six others and said, "Come here and be prepared to speak." I looked at my friend, the minister, and he had his mouth open. He had never seen such a thing.

And then I said, "Fellows, what shall we sing this morning?" And with one voice they said, "Come, Come, Ye Saints!" And I said, "Who can lead the music?" and most of them raised their hands. I selected one. "Who can play this portable organ?" And again there was a fine showing, and one was selected.

Now, we didn't have any books, but the man at the organ sounded a chord, and those young men stood, shoulders back and chins pulled in, and they sang all the verses of "Come, Come, Ye Saints." Now, I have heard that sung all over the Church many times, even by the Tabernacle Choir, to whom I apologize for what I am going to say. I have never heard "Come, Come, Ye Saints" sung with such fervor, such conviction, such power as those young men sang it. When they came to that last verse—"And should we die before our journey's through, happy

13

day, all is well"—I tell you it was thrilling. And as I looked at my friend again I found him weeping.

After the prayer, one of the boys knelt at the sacrament table, and he said, "Oh God, the Eternal Father . . ." and then he paused for what seemed to be a full minute before proceeding. At the close of the meeting, I went and looked him up. I put my arm across his shoulder and said, "What's the matter, lad?"

He said, "Why?"

"Well you seemed to have difficulty in asking a blessing on the bread. Has something happened?"

"Well sir," he said, "a few hours ago I was over Germany and France on a bombing mission. We had made our run, left our calling cards (meaning the bombs), and when we gained altitude and were about to return across the channel, we ran into heavy flak. My tail assembly was pretty well shot away, one of my engines was out, a number of my crew were wounded, and it looked like a hopeless situation. It seemed like no power in heaven or earth could get us back across the Channel to a landing field. But," he said, "Brother Brown, up there I remembered what my mother had said to me. (And this I want to say to this vast audience, both those that are here and those that are listening in.) This is what my mother said: 'If ever you find yourself in a situation where man can't help you, call on God.' I had been told that same thing in Primary, in the seminaries, in Sunday School: 'If ever you need help and man can't help you, call on God.' Although it seemed hopeless and impossible, I said, 'Oh God, the Eternal Father, please sustain this ship until we get back into England.' . . . Brother Brown, he did just that.

"When I heard of this meeting I ran all the way to get here, and when I knelt at the table and named his name again, I remembered shamefully that I had not stopped to say, 'thank you.' And that's the reason I paused, to express my gratitude for the goodness of God."

Well, we went on with our meeting and these young men spoke, and they spoke with power and conviction. Every one who heard them was thrilled by the evidence of their faith, and my friend, the chaplain, continued to weep. When they had

14

finished talking, I said, "Fellows, we'll have to dismiss." (That meeting was not like this; it had to be dismissed on time.) I said, "We'll have to dismiss or you won't get any chow."

They said, "We can have chow any time. Let's have a testimony meeting."

"Why," I said, "if you have a testimony meeting you'll be here another two hours."

They repeated with one voice, "Please let us have a testimony meeting."

I turned to my friend, the minister, and said, "Now I know this is unusual for you. We've been here two hours and we're going to be here another two hours. We'll excuse you if you prefer to withdraw."

He put his hand on my knee and said, "Please, Sir, may I remain?" And, of course, I encouraged him to stay, and then for two solid hours those young men, one after another, stood up and bore witness of the truth of the gospel. My only job was to say, "You're next, and then you, and then you," because all of them wanted to get up at once. It was a glorious occasion.

Finally there came an end. We dismissed, and this minster turned to me and said, "Mr. Brown, I have been a minister of the gospel for twenty-one years but this has been the greatest spiritual experience of my life." And again he said, "How do you do it? How did you know which of those fellows to call on?"

I replied, "It didn't make any difference which one I called on. They are all prepared. And this could happen in any camp anywhere in the world where there are seventy-five young Mormon boys."

I relate this to you, my dear students, that you may realize the value of participation—the value of a conviction of the truth —and that you may take advantage of every opportunity to bear witness to that truth.

---

("An Eternal Quest—Freedom Of The Mind," an Address given to the BYU Student Body, May 13, 1969.)

**HUGH B. BROWN**

## *"I Cannot Buy That with Money"*

I think I should not leave you this morning without bearing my testimony to you. I have no object in trying to deceive you. There is nothing to be gained by lying to you, and what I shall now say comes from the very center of my heart. It has to do with my convictions—convictions gained over a period of sixty to eighty years—convictions regarding myself, my sources, my destiny, my God and my relationship to him. I can say to you my young friends, that God has been so good to me as to give me an individual testimony of his Son, Jesus Christ. He is, in fact, the Son of the living God, the Redeemer of the world, its Savior. I know that to be true. I know it as I know of few other things in the world. May I just take a moment of your time to give you one incident to illustrate how I know it. This is a little unknown chapter out of my own life. It illustrates how I know that God lives.

We were in Canada. I was . . . an attorney for an oil company and a manager of it. We were drilling wells and making money. I was at the moment up in the Canadian Rockies, way back from the highways. We were drilling there. Everything looked very prosperous. I woke very early one morning before daylight. I was troubled in my mind, and I didn't know the source or the reason for the trouble. And I began to pray, but didn't seem to get an answer. And I remembered that the Savior was wont to go into the mountain tops frequently. You remember, his life was punctuated by mountain peaks. There is the mountain peak of the temptation, there is the mountain peak of the transfiguration, there is the mountain peak of the Beatitudes, there is the mountain peak from which he took flight into heaven. So thinking about this, I arose before daylight and went back up into the hills where I knew no one would be near. And when I got up on an advantageous point, I began to talk out loud. I was talking to God! Now, I do not mean that he was standing there listening to me or replying to me. But I mean from the very center of my heart I was calling to him.

Now my family were all in good health, all quite prosperous, and it looked as for myself that within a few days I would be a multi-millionaire. And yet, I was depressed. And up there on that mountain peak I said to him, "O God, if what it seems is about to happen will happen, and if it is not to be for the best good of myself and my family and my friends, don't let it happen. Take it from me." I said, "Don't let it happen unless in your wisdom it is good for me." Well, I left the mountains and came down to the camp. I got into my car and drove to the city of Edmonton. It was a Friday, and while I was driving I was thinking of what had happened. And I felt that there was something impending that I couldn't understand. When I arrived home, and after a bite to eat, I said to Sister Brown, "I think I'll occupy the back bedroom because I'm afraid I'm not going to sleep." Now I went in the bedroom alone and there, through the night, I had the most terrible battle with the powers of the adversary. I wanted to destroy myself. Not in the sense of suicide; but something within me was impelling me to wish that I could cease to be. . . . It was terrible. The blackness was so thick you could feel it.

Sister Brown came in later in the night, toward morning in fact, wanting to know what was the matter. And when she closed the door, she said, "What's in this room?" And I said, "Nothing but the power of the devil is in this room." And we knelt together by the bedside and prayed for release. We spent the night together, the balance of it. And in the morning I went down to my office. It was Saturday now and there was no one at the office. And in going into the office, I knelt by a cot and asked God for deliverance from the darkness that had enveloped me. And coming from somewhere there was an element of peace, the kind of peace that rests on the souls of men when they make contact with God. And I called her and said, "Everything is all right, or is going to be!"

That night at 10:00 o'clock, October 1953—the telephone rang. Sister Brown answered. She called me and said, "Salt

Lake's calling," and I wondered who could be calling me from that far away. I took the phone and said, "Hello." "This is David O. McKay calling. The Lord wants you to give the balance of your life to Him and His Church. We are in a conference of the Church. The concluding session will be tomorrow afternoon. Can you get here?"

I told him I couldn't get there because there were no planes flying, but I would get there as soon as possible. I knew that a call had come. And the call came after this awful conflict with the adversary. And when he said, "The Lord wants you to give the balance of your life to the Church," I knew that it meant giving up the money; it meant that I'd turn everything over to someone else and go to Salt Lake without monetary remuneration.

Since that time, I've been happier than ever before in my life. The men with whom I was associated have made millions. And yet, when one of them was in my office not long ago in Salt Lake, he said, "I am worth at least seven million dollars. I would gladly give every dollar of it to you if you could give me what you have. I can't buy it with money, but I'd like to have what you have. What you have is peace of soul, and I cannot buy that with money."

Brothers and sisters, I leave this testimony with you.

---

("Eternal Progression," an address to the student body of the Church College of Hawaii, October 16, 1964, pp. 8-10.)

---

## HUGH B. BROWN

---

## *"The Gardener and the Currant Bush"*

In the early dawn, a young gardener was pruning his trees and shrubs. He had one choice currant bush which had gone too much to wood. He feared therefore that it would produce little, if any, fruit.

Accordingly, he trimmed and pruned the bush and cut it back. In fact, when he had finished, there was little left but stumps and roots.

Tenderly he considered what was left. It looked so sad and deeply hurt. On every stump there seemed to be a tear where the pruning knife had cut away the growth of early spring. The poor bush seemed to speak to him, and he thought he heard it say:

Oh, how could you be so cruel to me; you who claim to be my friend, who planted me and cared for me when I was young, and nurtured and encouraged me to grow? Could you not see that I was rapidly responding to your care? I was nearly half as large as the trees across the fence, and might soon have become like one of them. But now you've cut my branches back; the green, attractive leaves are gone, and I am in disgrace among my fellows.

The young gardener looked at the weeping bush and heard its plea with sympathetic understanding. His voice was full of kindness as he said,

Do not cry; what I have done to you was necessary that you might be a prize currant bush in my garden. You were not intended to give shade or shelter by your branches. My purpose when I planted you was that you should bear fruit. When I want currants, a tree, regardless of its size, cannot supply the need.

No, my little currant bush, if I had allowed you to continue to grow as you had started, all your strength would have gone to wood; your roots would not have gained a firm hold, and the purpose for which I brought you into my garden would have been defeated. Your place would have been taken by another, for you would have been barren. You must not weep; all this will be for your good; and some day, when you see more clearly, when you are richly laden with luscious fruit, you will thank me and say, "Surely, he was a wise and loving gardener. He knew the purpose of my being, and I thank him now for what I then thought was cruelty."

Some years later, this young gardener was in a foreign land, and he himself was growing. He was proud of his position and ambitious for the future.

One day an unexpected vacancy entitled him to promotion. The goal to which he had aspired was now almost within his grasp, and he was proud of the rapid growth which he was making.

But for some reason unknown to him, another was appointed in his stead, and he was asked to take another relatively unimportant post, one which, under the circumstances, caused his friends to feel that he had failed.

The young man staggered to his tent and knelt beside his cot and wept. He knew now that he could never hope to have what he had thought so desirable. He cried to God and said, "Oh, how could you be so cruel to me? You who claim to be my friend—you who brought me here and nurtured and encouraged me to grow. Could you not see that I was almost equal to the other men whom I have so long admired? But now I have been cut down. I am in disgrace among my fellows. Oh, how could you do this to me?"

He was humiliated and chagrined, and a drop of bitterness was in his heart, when he seemed to hear an echo from the past. Where had he heard those words before? They seemed familiar. Memory whispered:

"I'm the gardener here."

He caught his breath. Ah, that was it—the currant bush! But why should that long-forgotten incident come to him in the midst of his hour of tragedy? And memory answered with words which he himself had spoken:

Do not cry . . . what I have done to you was necessary . . . you were not intended for what you sought to be, . . . if I had allowed you to continue . . . you would have failed in the purpose for which I planted you and my plans for you would have been defeated. You must not weep; some day when you are richly laden with experience you will say, "He was a wise gardener. He knew the purpose of my earth life. . . . I thank him now for what I thought was cruel."

His own words were the medium by which his prayer was answered. There was no bitterness in his heart as he humbly spoke again to God and said, "I know you now. You are the gardener, and I the currant bush. Help me, dear God, to endure the pruning, and to grow as you would have me grow; to take my allotted place in life and ever more to say, 'Thy will not mine be done.' "

Another lapse of time in our story. Forty years have passed. The former gardener and officer sits by his fireside with wife and children and grandchildren. He tells them the story of the currant bush—his own story; and as he kneels in prayer with them, he reverently says to God, "Help us all to understand the purpose of our being, and be ever willing to submit to thy will and not insist upon our own. We remember that in another garden called Gethsemane the choicest of all thy sons was glorified by submission unto thy will."

As they arose from prayer, this family group, they joined in singing a familiar hymn which now had for them new meaning.

"It may not be on the mountain height,
Or over the stormy sea;
It may not be at the battle's front
My Lord will have need of me. . . .

So trusting my all to thy tender care,
And knowing thou lovest me,
I'll do thy will with a heart sincere;
I'll be what you want me to be."

The father closed home evening with the lines:

"My will not thine be done," turned paradise into a desert.
"Thy will not mine," turned the desert into a paradise, and made Gethsemane the gate of heaven.

---

(Brown, Hugh B., *Eternal Quest.* [Salt Lake City: Bookcraft, 1956], pp. 243-46.)

# Biographical Sketch

## BISHOP VICTOR L. BROWN

$V$ictor L. Brown, second counselor in the Presiding Bishopric of The Church of Jesus Christ of Latter-day Saints, has had extensive experience in the Church and was an airlines executive prior to his high Church appointment.

Bishop Brown was born July 31, 1914, in Cardston, Alberta, Canada, a son of Gerald S. and Maggie Lee Brown. He attended the University of Utah, the Latter-day Saints Business College, and has taken extension work from the University of California.

His Church positions included ward Young Men's Mutual Improvement superintendent, bishop of the Denver Fourth Ward and counselor in the Denver Stake Presidency for six years, from 1954 until 1960.

Bishop Brown's experience with the airlines began in Salt Lake City in 1940. He then served as United Air Lines reservation manager in Washington, D.C., from 1943 until 1947, and reservation manager in Chicago for one year. In 1948 he became chief of payload control at Denver and in 1956 was named manager of space control. He held this position for five years until he was transferred to Chicago as assistant to the director of reservations.

Bishop Brown was called to the Presiding Bishopric in October 1961.

He is married to the former Lois Kjar of Salt Lake City, and they have five children: Victor L. Jr., Gerald E., Joanne K. Soderborg, Patricia L., and Stephen M.

# VICTOR L. BROWN

*"Bobby Polacio"*

Let me just share with you a story of a young boy whose Mexican mother taught him to be honest. I shall read it because if I were to tell it, I would miss something:

"Today I saw truth. For a moment I lived and breathed in the great presence of truth and felt its sweetness plunge deep into my soul.

"I am a coach in a junior high school. I work with 500 boys each day. This has been my occupation for over 20 years. I enjoy it.

"Traditionally, I am supposed to be rugged, tough, crusty; yes, even a little severe at times—and yet, underneath this exterior, feeling and understanding must exist if the job is to be done.

"Today was test day in climbing the rope. We climb from a standing start to a point 15 feet high. One of my tasks these past few weeks has been to train and teach the boys to negotiate this distance in as few seconds as possible.

"The school record for the event is 2.1 seconds. It has stood for three years. Today this record was broken. But this is not my story. How this record was broken is the important thing here, as it so often is in many an endeavor in this life.

"For three years Bobby Polacio, a 14½-year-old ninth grade Mexican boy, has trained and pointed and, I suspect, dreamed of breaking this record. It has been his consuming passion; it seemed his whole life depended upon owning this record.

"In his first of three attempts, Bobby climbed the rope in 2.1 seconds, tying the record. On the second try the watch stopped at 2.0 seconds flat, a record! But as he descended the rope and the entire class gathered around to check the watch, I knew I must ask Bobby a question. There was a slight doubt in my mind whether or not the board at the fifteen foot height had been touched. If he missed, it was so very, very close—not more than a fraction of an inch—and only Bobby knew this answer.

"As he walked toward me, expressionless, I said, 'Bobby, did you touch?' If he had said, 'Yes,' the record he had dreamed of since he was a skinny seventh-grader and had worked for almost daily would be his, and he knew I would trust his word.

"With the class already cheering him for his performance, the slim, brown-skinned boy shook his head negatively. And in this simple gesture, I witnessed a moment of greatness.

"Coaches do not cry. Only babies cry, they say. But as I reached out to pat this boy on the shoulder, there was a small drop of water in each eye. And it was with effort through a tight throat that I told the class: 'This boy has not set a record in the rope climb. No, he has set a much finer record for you and everyone to strive for. He has told the simple truth.'

"I turned to Bobby and said, 'Bobby, I'm proud of you. You've just set a record many athletes never attain. Now, in your last try I want you to jump a few inches higher on the take-off. You're going to break this record.'

"After the other boys had finished their next turns, and Bobby came up to the rope for his try, a strange stillness came over the gymnasium. Fifty boys and one coach were breathlessly set to help boost Bobby Polacio to a new record. He climbed the rope in 1.9 seconds! A school record, a city record, and perhaps close to a national record for a junior high school boy.

"When the bell rang and I walked away, now misty-eyed,

from this group of boys, I was thinking: 'Bobby, little brown skin, with your clear, bright, dark eyes and your straight, trim, lithe body—Bobby, at 14 you are a better man than I. Thank you for climbing so very, very high today.' "

(*Conference Report,* April, 1965, pp. 67-68. Permission granted, *Boy's Life.*)

## VICTOR L. BROWN

### *"Michael and Bill"*

Michael is now sixteen years of age. His parents were members of the Piute Indian tribe. Michael was born without his eyesight. On the Indian reservation, this was considered a terrible handicap. His family was very poor, and a blind boy was more than they could cope with. So, when Michael was about seven years old, he was left on the desert to die. Fortunately, some passing tourists found him and took him to a hospital. It took a year for the doctors and nurses to save his life and restore his health.

During this experience of being left on the desert all alone without food and water, unable to see, Michael's basic animal instincts for survival became so strong that he almost became an animal, fearing and hating everybody and everything. Eight years later, when I first met him, he told me he could remember the horror of being all alone—hungry, thirsty, and lost.

When he became well enough, Michael was sent to school. He was incorrigible. Because of his tragic experience, he destroyed everything he could get his hands on—paper, pencils, record player. Everything was his enemy. I suppose the school authorities despaired of ever reaching this boy. One day, they placed a call to a wonderful Latter-day Saint woman and asked her if she would mind taking an Indian boy into her home. She readily agreed.

Michael's nature had not changed. He still considered everyone his enemy. He continued to destroy almost everything that came in his way. One day one of the neighbor boys, a white boy by the name of Richard, became acquainted with Michael. Richard was bout fifteen years old. He was a teacher in the Aaronic Priesthood. He took an interest in Michael and fast became his friend.

Richard came to the Presiding Bishopric's Office one day and asked about the cost of the Book of Mormon in Braille. He had been saving his money for a long time so that he might purchase a Book of Mormon in Braille as a birthday present for his blind Indian buddy. The cost was more than Richard had saved. However, a kind person made it possible for him to obtain the book. As Michael read with his fingers, Richard followed along in his own Book of Mormon reading out loud, thus helping Michael over the more difficult words. As I visited with Michael, he said he had never read such wonderful stories. He said that everything he had read in the past was kid stuff, but the Book of Mormon was different. I asked him what the greatest desire of his heart was. This fifteen-year-old Indian boy replied: "To become sixteen years old so I can be baptized a member of The Church of Jesus Christ of Latter-day Saints." He explained that he must wait until his sixteenth birthday because of the requirement of the agency responsible for him.

Michael had his sixteenth birthday just this August and was baptized by his buddy, Richard, who is now a priest. Just four weeks ago, Michael was ordained a deacon in the Aaronic Priesthood by his foster father.

Michael told his mother that as he was being confirmed a member of the Church, the brightest feeling went through his entire body. He said, "I know now what 'white' looks like.' This sixteen-year-old Indian boy who has never seen the light of day now knows what "white" looks like. The Holy Ghost has borne witness to him.

This last school year, Michael, the boy who was incorrigible, was honored for his excellence in school effort—excellence in deportment, scholarship, and progress—the only boy so honored by his school this year. He hopes someday to teach other blind children as he has been taught.

Bill is not fifteen. His parents are Navajo. When Bill was a child, he was stricken with polio, which left him without the use of his legs. Bill and Michael are brothers in this foster home. They are both Boy Scouts. A year ago, they needed money to go to Scout camp, so they decided to sell toothbrushes and toothpaste. They didn't have much luck in their own neighborhood, so Michael pushed Bill in his wheelchair seven miles to another community where they had some success. They said that the most interesting and the funniest experience of the day was when they sold a toothbrush and some toothpaste to a man who didn't have any teeth.

Three weeks ago at a stake quarterly conference, I invited Bill to come to the front of the chapel and bear his testimony to over twelve hundred people. I wish you could have seen this fifteen-year-old Navajo Indian boy. Immaculate in his appearance and with all the dignity and majesty of a great chief, he sat in his wheelchair and humbly expressed his gratitude to his Heavenly Father for his many blessings, for his parents, his brothers and sisters, his membership in the Church, and the blessing of holding the office of teacher in the Aaronic Priesthood. Bill is a fine artist and hopes someday to become a great architect.

Bill and Michael have two lovely, blond, fair-skinned sisters and a baby brother, Ronnie. Let me tell you about Ronnie. As far as we know, he is also a Navajo Indian boy. When the agency called this same good mother and asked if she would take a three-year-old Indian baby into her home, they said that the child was totally incapacitated. He could not walk; he could not talk. They explained the outlook for him as almost hopeless. Notwithstanding this, she accepted him into her home. When I met Ronnie the other day, he had a mischievous twinkle in his eye and a smile on his face as he ran and tried to escape from one of his sisters—as normal a four-year-old as I have ever seen.

A blind boy, a crippled boy, a child who was a complete invalid—each one destined to a life of misery and hopelessness but for the love, compassion, charity, and understanding of a wonderful woman—a woman who wanted children more than anything else in the world and who was not blessed with any of her own. She wanted them so badly it didn't matter what their handicaps nor that their skin was copper color. The love she gave them was the love she had missed so desperately during her childhood. The compassion she blessed these children with was the compassion she longed for and sought but failed to find as she was growing up. To me she typifies the saint as described by Felix Adler as he makes the distinction between a hero and a saint. Paraphrasing this statement:

"The hero (heroine) is one who kindles a great light in the world, who sets up blazing torches in the dark streets of life for men to see by. The saint is the man (woman) who walks through the dark paths of the world, himself (herself) a 'light'."

(*Conference Report*, October 6, 1963, pp. 119-20.)

# Biographical Sketch

## ELDER PAUL H. DUNN

Elder Paul H. Dunn, a career Church educator and author, was named a member of the First Council of the Seventy April 6, 1964, during the 134th Annual General Conference of The Church of Jesus Christ of Latter-day Saints in Salt Lake City, Utah.

Elder Dunn was born in Provo, Utah, April 24, 1924, a son of Joshua Harold and Geneve Roberts Dunn. He was married to Jeanne Alice Cheverton on February 27, 1946. They are the parents of three daughters: Janet Dunn Gough, Marsha Jeanne, and Kellie Colleen.

He was graduated from Chapman College with an A.B. degree in religion in 1953, and received the M.S. degree in educational administration in 1954 at University of Southern California. He received his doctorate in the same field at U.S.C. in 1959.

Dr. Dunn is the author of three books.

Elder Dunn served as coordinator of LDS Institutes of Religion in Southern California for two years prior to his call to The First Council of the Seventy. He began his association with the Church's educational system in 1952 as a seminary teacher in Los Angeles.

An outstanding school athlete, Elder Dunn participated in baseball, football, basketball, golf, and track, and played professional baseball for four years before resuming his educational career.

# PAUL H. DUNN

---

*"A Call from the Prophet"*

The next voice I heard was that of our prophet. He came on very firmly, very kindly. He said, "Brother Dunn?" When I heard that, I came to full attention. "Yes, sir?"

He said, "How long would it take you to get to Salt Lake City?"

Well, I have a very peculiar mind. The way that my thought processes go, I tend oftentimes, without thinking any more than I do, to say things that need to be thought out more clearly. This was one of those occasions. I said, "President McKay, I am in Downey, sir. That's in California."

He then made what I thought was a very marvelous observation for a prophet. He came right back and he said, "I know that." I guess he did. He said, very gently again, "I'm asking you, how long would it take you to come to Salt Lake?"

I said, "Well, without checking into the schedules, I believe I could be there some time tomorrow."

He said, "That would be fine. I'll expect you in my office at eight o'clock tomorrow morning."

Well, my mind is still the inquisitive type. So I started to pursue a little bit, because I could tell he was ready to hang up. I said, "Well, what should I bring with me? Do you need my institute of religion reports?" I thought, "What has he discovered?" By then every sin I had ever committed had gone by. I needed to know how to defend myself.

He said, "No. Just bring yourself."

I said, "How about my wife?"

He said, "That would be lovely, if you could bring her."

"Anything else?"

"No," he said, "I'll see you in my office at eight o'clock tomorrow morning. Have a nice journey. Good-bye." And he hung up.

That is a traumatic thing. How do you go back into the kitchen and tell your wife that the Prophet wants to see you? I tried. She was just putting the final touches on the meal and was at the breadboard slicing the roast beef. Typical of all good American housewives, wanting to know what was the purpose of the call, she turned to me, and I will never forget that expression. She said, "Who was on the phone, dear?"

I said, "Oh, no one, just the Prophet." She about cut the breadboard in two.

Then to show you how much faith she had in me, the next observation she made, she said, "Well what did you do? What did you do?"

I said, "I don't know, but he wants to see us tomorrow morning at eight o'clock, and we had better get going."

Some of you who reside in Utah and the surrounding areas may appreciate the problem we were having with the weather here last April. I finally elected to drive because it was the only sure way of getting there at the appropriate hour. What a trip that was!

I pulled into Salt Lake about ten minutes before I was due. I left my wife with the Tingeys, very close friends of ours here in Provo, because the Prophet asked to see me alone.

I knocked on his hotel door, standing there wondering what must this entail. The door very quickly opened. One of the aides asked me to step in. I did. Getting just inside the doorway

I could see down the little corridor to my right into the room that had been made over into a little office for President McKay, where he could work in the hotel when his strength would not permit him to go over to the office.

He was sitting there very diligently at his work. He looked up and, noticing that I had arrived, he very quickly got up and took his cane—he was able to move without more aid than that at the time—and he hurried down that little corridor, laid his cane beside the wall, and extended his two hands in greeting to me. He said, as he looked into my eyes, "Brother Dunn, thanks so much for coming to Salt Lake to see me."

Imagine that! Talk about graciousness and respect! He was thanking *me* for coming to see *him*.

Then he turned to the other individual and said, "Will you see that Brother Dunn and I are not disturbed for the next hour?"

I remember thinking, "What in the world have we got to talk about for an hour?"

Then he very quickly and gently took me by the arm, cane in the other hand, and I was literally escorted back into his room. He was helping me; it was not the reverse.

As we got inside his office, he closed the door. Because I had a topcoat on, he turned me around—just moved me bodily —helped me off with my overcoat, put it over his arm, took it over and put it on the couch there in the room. He came back, and instead of putting me out in front in a typical counselee-counselor relationship, he asked me to take a chair beside him. Then he worked his way back around the desk and took his place in a little swivel chair. He turned it sideways so that we had this face-to-face contact, and he leaned back, just looking right through me as only he can do. With that wonderful smile on his face, he said, "Brother Dunn, tell me a little bit about yourself."

I couldn't even remember my name. I remembered vaguely I had a mother, so I started there and kind of worked back. I believe he enjoyed my fright and plight, just sitting there smiling very kindly.

After about twelve minutes of visiting—and, oh, does he

have an ability, those of you who have had this opportunity to stand and sit in his presence know, to make you feel good and at ease and the equal brother and sister that we are in the gospel setting.

As I sat experiencing this, he said, "I guess you are wondering why I have asked you to come to see me."

The thought had gone through my mind. I said, "Yes, sir."

He said, "Brother Dunn, last December, as you know, we lost a great Latter-day Saint in the passing of President Levi Edgar Young." He said, "I am calling you this morning to fill that vacancy."

When he said that, I had a feeling, and an impression come over me, like I have never experienced in my life. Spiritually I was just out of breath. Having played professional baseball for a number of years, I have been hit in the midsection my share of the time. You brethren who have been so involved—maybe some of you good sisters—know how difficult it is to get your wind. This is exactly what I was going through—just gasping for air. I believe he even enjoyed that as I watched him.

I made another comment that came out before I thought about it. Don't ever do this in his presence. I said, "President McKay, in all my life I have never once doubted your judgment or inspiration—until right now."

He did not lose his sense of humor entirely, but he came pretty close. He raised that finger and started to shake it at me a little bit, and he said, "Now, Brother Dunn, I don't want to hear of that any more." He said, "The Lord has called you to this position."

Then he went on for the next forty-seven minutes to interrogate and to investigate my soul through the process of diligent interviewing. . . .

At the conclusion of it, he stood up, which was my indication that the interview was over. He again extended his hands to me to take very warmly. As I did so, without any warning, he very quickly threw his arms around me and kind of pulled me close and held me there, just the way a father would do his son, or a grandfather his grandson, and did not say a word. But, oh, the spirit that radiates from a living prophet as you are in close physical communication one with another! Talk about a testimony being verified! Latter-day Saints, there is a living prophet if I have ever known one.

---

"A Call from the Prophet," an address given to the BYU student body October 20, 1964.)

---

## PAUL H. DUNN

### "A Missionary Inquires"

Nephi tells us to inquire of the Lord. Let me just share a quick experience in this connection. I have just come from the mission field and so this is fresh on my mind. I have got a little elder out in New England that by all physical standards should not have come on a mission. He is eighty per cent deaf in one ear and seventy per cent deaf in the other. He has a terrible speech impediment because he has never heard his own voice clearly. But ever since he was at his mother's knee he has desired to go on a mission. You know you get lots of missionaries that come out for the right reason—to do the right thing for the right reason. Then occasionally you get one or two that come to do a good thing for the wrong reason. Hopefully we can give even them the vision and help them catch the spirit.

But this little elder came to do the Lord's work—the right thing for the right reason—and nothing was to stay his hand. Well, he has been out about a year now. About two months ago on one of our preparation days—and although try as we do to give them counsel not to get over-involved in physical activities —they were out playing some touch football with the other missionaries of the district. We have a 270-pound elder that was in the same district, and he went up to block a pass and this little semi-deaf elder was underneath him. As the 270-pound elder came down, he crashed upon his head, causing instant deafness in the elder.

His companion called me that night. He said, "President Dunn, we have a problem. Elder So-and-so can't hear. He has lost his hearing in a little accident today on the ball field." So I suggested they bring him to Cambridge where we have the Massachusetts General Hospital and all the services of the Harvard Medical School. We put him in touch with two of the finest ear specialists, I guess, known to the world, and after an extensive examination, the report came back: "He will not regain his hearing."

So I brought the elder into my office and we were trying to decide now what was best for him. Do you send him home? What do you do? He could barely hear me so we were writing notes to each other. And as I was sharing with him some of my feelings, he wrote me a note. I'll never forget it. "You believe in God don't you, President Dunn?"

And I wrote back, "Yes, elder, you know I do."

Then he gave me in the little note, almost verbatim, the counsel of Nephi, "Would you inquire of the Lord, because I came to serve a mission?"

I wrote back, "Certainly."

So we knelt down together after I closed the door and locked it. I put my arm around his shoulder. He couldn't hear the prayer too well, I guess, except through the Spirit. I asked my Heavenly Father to give me the strength and the courage and the know-how to touch the life of this young man. I felt impressed in that prayer to give him a special blessing of health, so we rose together and I seated him in a chair and still he could hardly hear me. I placed my hands upon his head and called upon my Heavenly Father by the authority and power of the priesthood which I hold and in the name of our Savior, Jesus Christ. I paused momentarily and then as forcefully as I have ever felt an impulse from heaven, I promised him that he would hear again—and so commanded it. It wasn't immediate. We stood together and embraced each other, tears were in both of our eyes. He wrote back on a little note, "Send me back to my area, I'll be all right. The Lord has spoken to my soul."

I sent him back to new Hampshire. The next morning the telephone rang—"Dear President Dunn, just thought you would like to know I got my hearing back last night."

"Have ye inquired of the Lord?" is what Nephi counseled us. Today, as I have indicated, there are some in this congregation that are disturbed, who have great concern, whether it be for life generally, marriage, the military, or schooling. Whatever the dilemma, could I counsel you, my young brothers and sisters, to take it to the Lord.

---

(*BYU Speeches of the Year,* "Have Ye Inquired of the Lord?" April 8, 1969, pp. 10-12.)

---

PAUL  H.  DUNN

### "A Tribute to the Church"

The presidency of the university, in being the genial hosts they are, provided a very fine luncheon just prior to our conference presentations. I noticed, as I stepped into the dining area, that I had been placed right beside a man in full Navy uniform, a commander by rank. We had never met. As we took our places—they were so identified by the little place cards—he turned to me. He had no way of knowing, except perhaps for a clue or two that I had given him, that I was a Mormon. He said, "Mr. Dunn, I would like to get acquainted with you." We shook hands and he said, "You're the Latter-day Saint, aren't you?"

I thought, "Good heavens! What have I done to tip my hand already?" I said, "Yes. How did you know?"

He said, "I noticed that you are not going to partake of that liquid." I had turned my cup over. There was the clue. I immediately, as we frequently do almost mechanically, started to defend my position. He said, as he interrupted me very quickly, "Look, I didn't inquire about your background to get a defense of your position." I then asked him why and he said, "I wanted to take this opportunity to salute you, sir. May I?"

Now I was just a PFC in World War II. For you ladies, that isn't very high. It is about as low as you can go. Any time a Navy commander wants to salute a private, I am not going to stop him. So I turned to him and said, "Yes, sir. Please go ahead."

Then he kind of hurt my ego a little. He said, "Well, I don't mean you, personally. I mean the organization that you are representing today—the great Latter-day Saint faith."

I was very inquisitive. I wanted to know why he had singled us out. As we sat down, I inquired, too. I said, "Why do you pay tribute to my church?"

He said, "Very simple. In my assignment as a Navy Commander I am in charge of the testing program for the United States Navy. But even prior to this I had an opportunity to travel all over the world. I have watched you people with keen interest." He was a sharp, capable leader, himself. He said, "Mr. Dunn, I don't know what it is about you people, but you have something that gets through to me. It's an air of confidence; it's an ideal; it's something that I can't quite put my hands on; but I'm convinced, sir, that one day this country—in fact, this world—will look to you people for spiritual direction. I want to take this opportunity as a family man, as an educator, and as a member of the armed forces, to salute you, sir, and your church for their wonderful standards and spiritual truths. It gives us all a sense of well-being just to know that such an organization exists."

Can you appreciate a little how proud I felt inside, with you, because individuals of this caliber know what you are? I thought as he gave us this tribute, "What a responsibility we each have to not only measure up, but to assume adequately the positions that our Heavenly Father has placed upon us to go and assist the world in becoming, literally, the kingdom of God."

_____

(Education Week Devotional, "Blessed Are the Teachable," June 8, 1964, pp. 11-12.)

_____

## PAUL  H.  DUNN

### "A New Ball Glove"

Let me share a brief experience of a priesthood father, my own. When I was about two years old, my family moved to the southern states, and there I spent the early part of my life. This was during the depression, and things were hard; but, fortunately for us, the Dunn family had it reasonably easy. My father was well paid for his labor. I remember, as a young, aspiring athlete, wanting to approach Dad on one occasion for a new ball glove; and being the child psychologist that I was, I knew that timing was everything. I plotted and schemed for the right moment to approach him, and it finally came.

I heard him come into the driveway and slam the car door and enter the house quickly. He entered the house whistling. That was always a good sign. My mother unknowingly had helped me to set the stage by fixing one of his favorite meals.

After dinner was over he had occupied his usual rocking chair and picked up the paper. I let him get through the heavy part, knowing that that was not a good time to inerrupt, and then I tiptoed in at the appropriate moment. I had an old worn-out mitt that wouldn't see me through another game, and I thought certainly he would understand my needs and would give the money without question. Well, I held the glove behind me, and as I stood looking at my father, I said, "Dad, how are you feeling?"

He assured me he was in good shape.

I said, "You have always taught your boys that whenever you do a thing in this life, you ought to do it right. Is that correct?"

He said, "That's right. I am glad you know it."

I said, "You have always taught us that when you do a job, you need the best equipment. Is that right?"

"That's right. I am glad that got through."

And then I said, "Whenever your boys perform, you have taught us to give it the best we had. Is that right?"

He said, "That is exactly right."

"All right," I said, "that is the reason I am here, sir. I want to show you something," and I brought the glove out.

He said, "Good heavens, what is it?"

I said, "It is a ball glove, and I need a new one. It will only cost $7.50 and I need the money right now. I have a big game Friday night and I am to pitch. If you will give me the money I'll be on my way and we'll both be happy."

He reached in his pocket and took out his pencil and his little notebook, and then I knew I had lost the battle. He went to work figuring. The going rate at that time for a boy my age was, I think, something like ten cents an hour. He said, "Why, Paul, that will only cost you seventy-five hours of labor." And I thought, how can a man be that cruel?

And so we went to work figuring out projects, and sure enough some four or five weeks later when I turned in my work slips, I was handed the $7.50 that I had earned. I remember going down to select that ball glove, and as I put it on my hand, I patted the pocket for just the right fit. I bought a ten-cent can of linseed oil in order to put it in proper shape.

I learned a great lesson that day. Of all the gloves I had ever owned, that glove was never left in the rain or for someone else to care for. I was a proud young man, but more specifically, young priesthood bearers, I began to see the point of a "welfare" dad and the principles he taught. The time has now come when my father isn't with me anymore, but the principles he taught remain, and I will always be able, I think, to stand and look the world in the eye because a dad cared.

(*Conference Report*, April 8, 1967, pp. 91-92.)

## PAUL H. DUNN

### *"I Had Really Earned My Letter"*

May I just share quickly one other experience. (Don't let this get any further, but I suppose this is the one part that *will* get out.) I was sitting in my little study at home and reminiscing with some old books and school records. (Do you ever do this—go through an old picture album, an old diary or something, and vicariously relive the past? Well, you are too young, you haven't had that much go past yet.) The time will come when you will find a great joy in reminiscing. I was doing just this, and, as I was cleaning out a file that contained some old documents, lo and behold, I came upon two Aaronic Priesthood awards given me some twenty-plus years ago. They had gold seals attached and you would normally think that a young priesthood bearer would be proud to have these in his possession, wouldn't you? That is true, if it truly represented what he had earned.

Now this is the part—unbeknownst even to my wife and daughters, I slipped into an area of our basement and burned both of those awards. I am sorry to have to tell you that today, my fellow brothers and sisters, because I hadn't *really* earned them and the fear entered my heart that the time might come when my own wife or children might one day discover them and think they were honorably won. Lest that happen, I destroyed the evidence, because you see it goes back into an era when I went through the mechanics of gospel living—not real living—only the motions. I let them put stars on my forehead and an award insignia on my lapel, but they were for complying with the mechanics, not for qualifying spiritually. Can you appreciate what I am trying to say? So I destroyed the awards.

Contrast that experience if you will with another experience that same night. As I continued to clean our records and books, I stepped over to the closet where some materials were located and, as I opened up the closet, in the shadows I could see my old high school letterman sweater hanging there. Can you appreciate, some of you athletes, what a bit of reminiscing that this brought to mind! I took it out and because I suppose this is the human side of people, I put it on. It was a bit snug here and there. I didn't dare let my family see me in it for fear they wouldn't understand.

I stood in front of the mirror. Here in front was the big block "H" from Hollywood High, and it had some interesting insignia attached which signified I was somebody—some stripes around the left sleeve—white on that beautiful maroon background. I stood there with real pride. I thought, "Isn't that great!" Do you know why? Because *I had really earned my letter,* and that letterman's sweater has a significant place in my heart.

Let me just conclude by telling you why. During the 1942 baseball season we in the Western Athletic Association had a real contest going. Hollywood High, my team, and Fairfax High, who were arch rivals, were battling it out for the city championship. We closed the season one game behind Fairfax with two games to go, and—wouldn't you know it—they both were to be played against Fairfax. I drew the starting assignment to pitch the second-to-the-last game. Well, I had the usual butterflies, you know how it is—couldn't sleep, couldn't think, couldn't study, couldn't do anything.

The day before the crucial game, Coach Meb Schroeder had us all assembled on the ball field. As we stood around the batting cage getting last minute instructions and the old pep talk, we were reminded of the standards and the oaths we had taken as athletes earlier in the year. Schroeder, even though he was not a member of the Church, held a very tight rein and demanded high standards. We had each committed ourselves to no smoking, no drinking, or staying out at night. He was building character in boys, not just teams or statistics. We took that commitment, and each of us promised we would obey; and we knew the penalties if we disobeyed.

As he made his way around the circle that day on the field he happened to glance over to where Jimmy Daniels, our star second baseman, was standing (batting .382—and for you sisters, that is a pretty good average, it really is). He was the Maury Wills of our team. He was the take-charge guy. He was the one that, when you had two men on base and only one out and things really were falling apart, could mold the team together.

The coach said, "Jimmy, is that a nicotine stain on your finger?"

Jimmy said, "Yes, sir."

He said, "Don't you know the rule?"

"Yes, sir."

He said, "Do you know the penalty?"

"Yes."

"You see the gym?"

"Yes, sir."

"Turn your uniform in right now. You are through."

The team was stunned. I almost hollered, "Coach, wait until *tomorrow!* We've got a game to win and we *need* Jimmy!" You know, isn't that the way we sometimes look at it? It doesn't matter what we are doing to people, but let's just *win, win!*

I have never seen a more dejected figure than Jimmy that day, walking toward the gym. But Schroeder was the kind of coach that didn't let a boy flounder. He worked with him all the more, even though he had lost his privilege to be on the team.

The next day on the Fairfax diamond we went into the bottom half of the thirteenth inning before they squeezed across run number one, which was the deciding run that beat us, 1 to 0. Would it surprise you if I told you that I bawled all night? That was a hearbreaker to lose for any pitcher.

Twenty years have come and gone and, do you know what is interesting about life, *I don't remember* who was on the top of the standing those many years ago, who batted what, where, when; but *I do remember* a great coach who taught me to discipline self.

So, as I occasionally look in the closet and see my letterman's sweater, I say, "Thank you, Meb Schroeder, wherever you are, for letting me know that the really important things in life are principles and standards—not records." This is what I found *true* happiness to be. I have come to know it, not in winning—sure it is great to win. But it is still greater to find the joy and peace and the serenity that come in truly living standards and principles of the gospel. I think that is what the scriptures are all about, and when applied to the everyday things of life, true joy is experienced.

<hr>

(*BYU Speeches of the Year*, "Happiness Is . . .," April 18, 1967, pp. 9-12.)

<hr>

**PAUL  H.  DUNN**

<hr>

## *"You Don't Look Like What You Are Supposed to Be"*

That is what Nick Cullup, my former manager in the old Pioneer League, did to me. While I would not want to follow some of his personal habits, he was an enthusiastic, effective manager. Three of us reported as rookies on the same day. He looked us over and said, "You fellows are supposed to be ball players?"

"Yep!" I showed him all my news clippings.

He wasn't impressed, "You don't *look* like what you are supposed to be."

(Great principle! "You don't *look* like what you are supposed to be." You don't radiate that confidence.)

He continued, "Kid, when I put you on a ball field, I want you to *look* like something. You don't know how to dress; you don't know how to walk; you don't know how to project yourself. Why, the opposing batters will have a field day on you! You have to learn to look mean and confident as well as skillful."

Time won't permit me to relate all the antics Nick put me through, but he taught me how to dress one day in front of a mirror: how to tuck my shirt in so that I looked like what I was supposed to be; how to beak the old cap; how to stand out on the mound and look mean at the batter. It is all a part of radiating enthusiasm.

He was an old catcher himself, from way back with the Washington Senators. His hands were knotted like the knots on a tree. That first day he walked out and said to me, "Kid, what's your best pitch?"

"Well," I said, "I can throw a fast ball and a good curve."

Then, without a catcher's mitt, he said, "Throw it to me. Give it all you've got."

I threw it—Pow!—and he said, "Is that *all* the harder you can throw?" (Now that really builds confidence, doesn't it?) He said, "I wouldn't mind if you played ball in my living room; you wouldn't hurt anything."

The need to radiate—he said, "I'm gonna help you." He had made a big overstuffed catcher's mitt, which looked like something Al Shaulk would carry out on the ball field. Nick used to soak this mitt in linseed oil. Then he'd bake it and get it just so it was crisp. Every time you would even throw a slow ball—POW!—that thing would pop.

"Now, when we get out on the field," he explained, "we're going to make you *sound* like what you're supposed to be. You're going to *radiate,* and the opponent is going to be so nervous that he will drop fifteen percent of his batting average when he sees you on the mound."

He taught me how to walk on to the field, how to look,

how to observe, how to make the ball sound like it was moving twice as fast as it was—WHAM! The opponent soon got the message. Enthusiasm is what Nick Cullup taught me, and that's the key to success. You radiate what you are!

(*BYU Speeches of the Year*, "Keys to Successful Living," February 13, 1968, pp. 15-16.)

PAUL  H.  DUNN

*"Lou Brisse"*

You students are now in the preparatory stage of life. Whether you are planning marriage or a profession, do you have the ingredient of education? Unless you are committed to your cause, your reaping of the happiness and success harvest will be nil. To be sure, dedication is a basic ingredient of a successful life.

I don't know how many of you will remember Lou Brisse, former pitcher of the Philadelphia Athletics some years ago. Most of you were still blessing the pre-existence when he broke into baseball. Here was a young man who had commitment, that dedication—a southpaw pitcher who signed with the Athletics. I happen to have gone into professional baseball the same year Lou did. We were of comparable age, graduating from high school at the same time.

Lou was a competitor's competitor. He was a hungry ball player, as we used to say. He wanted to go to the top, and he was committed to doing it. Well, as many of us may know, 1942 was a bleak period. That was when World War II really started to spread, and eighteen-year-olds were being drafted.

Lou was one of these. I didn't know much about him. I remember his name being talked about over in the spring training camps as a comer, a real competitor. Lou went over to Italy, to Sicily with the infantry. I got lost in the Pacific and didn't hear much about him. But his story came out a little later. On one of the beachheads he got hit in the right leg with a fragment from an 88 shell; it nearly took his leg off. He lay on the beach literally bleeding to death. In a semi-conscious state, he heard one of the field doctors say, "We'll have to take his leg off."

He gained just enough strength to say, "No! Please leave it on. I've got to earn a living as a ball player. Leave it, even though it is lifeless."

The doctor complied, "We will do what we can."

Back to the field hospital he went. After operations they put a steel plate in his leg and sent him home for fifty-three more operations. You would think that would discourage most people in this world—even with the gospel—wouldn't you? And Lou didn't have the gospel. Finally, in 1946 he was set free from his medical labors. He limped with a cane and reported back to Connie Mack and the Philadelphia ball club: "Connie, can I have my job back? The government says that's the arrangement."

Connie looked at his leg and with little hope said, "You can come and play with us."

So that year Lou worked out with the Athletics. In the spring of 1947 I happened to be in the training camp just a couple of fields away from where Lou was playing. They let him suit up that year. He went out with a bit of a limp, and through a rugged training program, he got himself into shape. To make a long story short, on opening day at Fenway Park, old Connie Mack walked out with that brand new baseball and handed it to him and said, "Lou, you have earned the right to start the game today." Lou walked out on the mound. If you have ever known the thrill of a lifetime to see a man come back, this is the example.

Lou got the first two batters out without any trouble. The third hitter that day was Ted Williams. Ted Williams was no slouch. I know; I have pitched to him a time or two, and if you ever want a lesson in humility, that's it! As he leveled off that bat, Ted hit the third pitch—a screaming line drive right back to the pitcher's box. It caught Lou on the right leg where the steel plate was embedded and threw him to the ground. He lay writhing on the mound, screaming in agony. I suppose some of you might be able to contemplate the pain. At that point, most people would quit, saying, "Why do I get all the problems?" "I'm discouraged. I'll throw in the towel." Not Lou Brisse. No, he was committed to a cause. He had a purpose in life. And, without the gospel of Jesus Christ, he crawled to his knees as old Connie Mack walked out to him and said, "Give me the ball, Lou. We'd better not take any more chances."

Lou objected. "Don't take me out. You know how long I have had to fight to come back."

"Sure, we know. Think you can get up on your feet?"

"Yes, sir."

With pain I suppose we can't measure, Lou stood and threw the next pitch. He finished that inning and the next. Finally, in the bottom half of the ninth inning, the score read: Philadelphia 4, Boston 2. It is one of the great comeback stories of all time. Eighteen wins he registered that year, because he would not quit. He had that commitment, that dedication to a great cause.

That is what makes a success, young people. Not quitting—stay down when you fall and you are a loser. Get up one more time and you will win. There is no disgrace in falling; it is lying there that defeats us. The life of every great person is full of discouragement—falling, failing. Getting up is what makes the winner. I love the life of that man who has taught me a great deal in this area of commitment.

---

(*BYU Speeches of the Year,* "Keys To Successful Living," February 13, 1968, pp. 7-9.)

---

## *"I Might Get HIM as a Son-in-Law!"*

**M**ay I make one other observation as it relates to my own family. My wife is a convert to the Church. She has great faith and is committed to gospel principles. I would only hope and pray that you as young Latter-day Saints, be it working with the non-Latter-day Saint element or with those who are not active, that you are more adept as a missionary than I was at the time I was pursuing Jeanne.

I used to frequent her house like most boys do when they are in pursuit. In fact, one year Dr. Cheverton, my father-in-law-to-be, indicated to me he had almost taken me as an income tax deduction because I had eaten so often in his home. I recall on one particular occasion when we were having a family dinner, that Mrs. Cheverton had set a beautiful table and we were in the process of eating when Dr. Cheverton, who was one of the great speakers of his generation and a Bible scholar, turned to me and asked, "Paul, tell me (I was a great mature lad of 18 at the time), what do the Mormons say about *first, second, third,* and *fourth* Isaiah?" (He was preparing a paper at the time on the Isaiah problem.) I hadn't even heard of the *first* one!

Now get this; this ought to thrill you as a missionary! I said, "I don't know, sir, but you're wrong and we're right!"

Now I trust that you have more empathy and understanding with your nonmember friends than I had. I remember looking at Dr. Cheverton and seeing in him the great fear, "I might get *him* as a son-in-law!"

---

(*BYU Speeches of the Year,* "Happiness Is . . . ," April 18, 1967, pp. 2-3.)

---

PAUL H. DUNN

## *"Yes, Sir"*

As one banker in the Chase-Manhattan organization said, "The primary problem with the college graduate of today is that he knows too much." If we could move into our fields of endeavor with the attitude of willingness to serve, to give, and to receive in terms of counsel—there is the man that will be at the top in a short time.

May I just illustrate this very quickly. I remember about three or four weeks after we had our grand opening at the particular supermarket I managed, I was plagued with applications for employment. It was a hard time in the late 1940's and it was obvious that there were fewer jobs than the number of people seeking them.

I got a telephone call one afternoon from a sixteen-year-old high school boy. He was very much to the point—very polite— and radiated just enough self-confidence so that I wanted to listen for a moment. He used the right terminology—"Yes,sir," and he let me take the lead—not that that was important, but it made me want to hear him. I have often watched this point of courtesy with great interest in the mission home, for example, and particularly on the day when we set these wonderful young people apart to go forth to teach the gospel. It is rare day, and I wish you could watch the brethren at the front of the room start to hum and buzz and whisper with each other when a young man with some competence can stand and look them in the eye and say, "Yes, sir," or "No, sir." Joseph Fielding Smith, our beloved President of the Council of the Twelve, directs and coordinates this meeting. Frequently he has to ask a personal question, like, "What does the 'N' stand for in your middle name? Is that 'N' another name?" Often as he asks the question the boy won't look up. He will reply, "Naw, naw," instead of saying, "No sir, it's just an initial." We cannot find two missionaries out of one hundred who are this courteous. It concerns us because it says, in essence, this is the type of attitude they are going to take to the rest of the world as they present the divine gospel.

To get back to my telephone conversation with the high school boy—the young man said, "Mr. Dunn, you don't know me." This was clever, I thought. He said, "I have watched with great interest the opening of this fine market in our community. My mother has been a constant shopper there ever since, and she is delighted!" I don't know how delighted she was, but I was ready to hear more.

He said, "I realize that you probably have all of your positions filled, but I believe I have something that will help your business. At a time that is convenient to you, sir, I would like to present my credentials. May I?" A sixteen-year-old boy!

I wanted to hear more about it. I said, "How about Wednesday afternoon after school?"

"Yes, sir, I'll be there." So I set it for four o'clock.

At one minute to four here came this young man—properly dressed, with a certain amount of confidence in his walk. I am sure he was scared to death. He probably had more butterflies than most of us have as he approached this interview. I thought then, as I watched this little episode unfold, "Wouldn't it have been marvelous if our deacon's quorum, our teachers and priests, could have even dressed like this on Sunday and walked in with equal competence and commitment!"

As we walked into the office I had him take a seat and I pulled up a chair beside him. I said, "Tell me just a little bit about yourself."

He did. He said, "I have had one job as a box boy on Saturdays. I believe I know enough of the business to be an asset to your organization. Mr. Dunn, I don't expect you to hire me here and now, but because I do have some ability, I'd like to prove it to you."

He said, "May we step out into the store for just a moment?"

I said, "Why, certainly."

So we did, and he took me over to the wall where all the canned goods were lined up. In opening the store we were having a difficult time keeping them properly stocked. He said, "Now Mr. Dunn, I think you know enough about sales appeal and the intuition of women as they shop around in a store to realize that if that shelf could always look full and properly aligned, I believe you could even double the sales." He said, "I'm the greatest man in the world in terms of keeping that shelf stocked. I don't expect you to believe it. You even look a little doubtful"—words to this effect. "Would you be willing to let me invest one week of my time every afternoon after school and all day Saturday to show you what I can do? And you have no obligation, sir."

What do you imagine I was thinking? I had at that time fifteen part-time box boys, Saturday boys, and they were all the "let-s'see-what-time-we-can-get-out-of-here-boys"—and the kids would gather at the counter, and here would come their friends. They were more concerned about acceptance with the peer group (which is important) than they were about what they could give to a business. They had the capacity, but they lacked the will to serve and to give of themselves.

Now, if you were managing a store, which element would you want, brothers and sisters? Do I have to tell you what I did? He worked that one afternoon. I had him take his coat off and show me. I didn't need to watch him very long. I let three boys go the next Saturday because this young man could fill all three positions.

Was the opportunity there? You bet. He had the ability; but, more important, he had the will to give and to serve and to show to the world in an unselfish way what he could do.

Who do you think got the consistent raise? Who do you think I made openings for in the future as the store volume dropped and settled to normal? Who do you think was going to succeed in college? Who do you think is going to the top in business with an attitude like this? There is no question, is there?

---

(Brigham Young University Summer School Devotional, "Three Basic Ingredients for Success," July 20, 1965, pp. 12-14.)

PAUL   H.   DUNN

*"Give Me a New Thought"*

**I** thought as Brother Webb was praying of one of the greatest advisers that walked into our lives when we were priests. His name was Charles B. Stewart. He is the father of Ike Stewart, the president of the Salt Lake Tabernacle Choir. I suppose he was late in his seventies when he was assigned by the bishop of the Hollywood Ward to be our adviser. And you know what a seventy-year-old man looks like to sixteen-year-olds. I thought Moses had returned. And we weren't about to give him much of a chance—sometimes we were a little cruel the way many teen-agers are.

I'll never forget the first morning we went up to our priests' class. Brother Stewart was standing at the door, not in the room, greeting his boys. There were six of us, as I recall, in that little quorum. He stopped us one by one as we made ready to enter into the room. And when it came my turn he said, "You're Paul Dunn, aren't you?"

"Yes, sir."

And he told me a little bit about myself. "Now," he said, "We have a requirement in this priests' class. You can't enter until you give me a thought." He said, "Have you got one?"

I hadn't had one in ten years, but he insisted, "We want a new thought." And I couldn't give him one. So he said, "All right, I'll teach you one. Now, you repeat after me, 'Attention is the mother of memory.' " And I stumbled through it and gave it back to him. He said, "That's fine, young man, you may enter my class." And I remember Francis had to give one too. I don't remember what his first line was but that was mine, "Attention is the mother of memory."

We had a fine class. We were a little disturbing to him at times, I'm sure, I remember he had long, bony fingers. I'll never forget he used to seat us in a semicircle around his feet.

He would walk back and forth and Francis and I used to frog each other once in a while. (That doesn't shake your faith, does it? You look at the size of him—I still wear a bruise from it!) He would come along that row and say, "Now, young men, we have invited the Lord to be with us today and he expects our attention. Remember, 'Attention is the mother of memory.' "

And I'll never forget one day as that finger came down the row, he said, "You realize, young men, that you are the future leaders of the Church?" He continued, "Why in this very circle there may be a future General Authority." And we all laughed. I remember when my call came, some of them were still laughing.

Well, the class period ended. We shaped up a little bit and went to go out, and he stopped me at the door and he said, "You can't leave until you give me another new thought." I didn't have one, and so he taught me another. He said, "Remember, Paul, 'A strong man and a waterfall always channel their own path.' Now repeat it back to me." And I did. He said, "You may go."

The following week I came to class and once more he said, "Do you have another new thought?"

"No, sir." So he taught me another.

I still recall it: "Example sheds a genial ray which men are apt to borrow, so first improve yourself today and then your friends tomorrow." I had a little trouble giving that one back, but he helped me as he did all of his boys.

Soon the class ended and he said, "Have you got a new thought?"

"No, I haven't."

"I'll teach you another, 'There was a wise old owl that sat in an oak, the longer he sat the less he spoke. The less he spoke the more he heard. Oh! Why can't we be like that wise old bird?' " Then he told us that he called these sayings "gem thoughts" and that the time would come in our lives when we would want to draw upon these ideas to help us in our lives. "One day you will find their true meaning."

"Paul," he'd say, " 'A good name is better than a girdle of gold.' Remember that!" Well, we left his class finally, after almost two years of association. I can testify to you the impact of his example still remains.

I was on the island of Okinawa, May of 1945, when I received a letter from Mrs. Stewart, and attached to the letter was a little obituary column announcing the passing of Charles B. Stewart, my adviser, my friend, my teacher. And honor to his name, in his concluding week of life he had typed a fresh page of "gem thoughts" for one of his priests who was fighting a great battle far away. I still carry the list with me, brothers and sisters, and so I admonish you to listen carefully to these great leaders and teachers.

I know some of you get a little discouraged at times when things aren't always going just the way they ought—pressures of the moment, great decisions to make, lots of other complications—but listen while you can because I promise you the hour will come in your life when you will draw upon these great words of wisdom as you make greater decisions in the future.

Since my days with Charles B. Stewart I have become a collector of "gem thoughts." One of these days if I get the inspiration I think I'll compile them for you. I have many thousands because he taught me to think new thoughts.

(*BYU Speeches of the Year*, "Have Ye Inquired of the Lord?," April 8, 1969, pp. 3-5.)

**PAUL H. DUNN**

### *"The New Testament Really Works"*

Some time ago I had a challenge as a father when one of my daughters, during her junior high school days, came to me with a social problem which was very disturbing. My daughter at the time was involved with a social group consisting of seven girls (four members of the Church and three nonmembers). The four had a silent pact, as it were, to try to convert the other three. As they were lunching together, as they frequently did, one of the young Latter-day Saint girls commenced to tell an off-color story. It was in poor taste, and totally out of order.

My daughter came home that night and recounted the situation; in fact, she was even bold enough to tell me the story. It was a problem! "Now," she said, "Dad, don't tell me what's right and what's wrong. I think I understand the principles of the gospel sufficiently to know that that wasn't the thing to do. But," she said, "What do you *do* when you find yourself in this kind of situation? How do you handle it?"

She didn't add this postscript, but I could see it in her eyes: "Remember, Dad, the important thing at my age is to be included. And remember, sir, any fifteen-year-old wants to be popular, to be accepted, to be wanted, and they don't want things to be too 'churchy!' " She was saying, in effect, "Will you give me an answer, and at the same time, keep me popular." Well, now, that *is* a task for any teacher or parent.

So we visited for a while and time won't permit all the details. I try frequently to get my daughters to see the principles of the gospel and their application to life. I turned, after some discussion, to the cleansing of the temple experience recorded in Matthew, Mark and Luke. You will recall the story of the Pharisees, the Sadducees, and the practices of the money changers. (I didn't take a lot of time to give her the history or background, although there are times when the history is needed and helpful. Somehow she could still live in this life without all of the excess baggage, as it were. Oh, I am not trying to suggest that these things aren't important to know historically, but more important than knowing the dimensions of the Nauvoo Temple, more important than knowing how many missions we have in the Church, more important than knowing what exactly will occur in the millennial reign, is *the ability to apply divine principles* daily so that life can be happy and truly enjoyed.) So as I read the cleansing of the temple story, I asked her, "What do you get out of this story?"

She said, "Well, the Savior was upset."

I said, "May I suggest one thought. He was saying to His peer group that there comes a time in every person's life when he has to stand up and be counted; and while it may not be the popular thing to do, there are times when you have to do what's right even though it isn't easy. You may have to stand alone a few times."

I said, "You think about that. Then you and I will have another talk."

She thought about it and came back a little while later and said, "I can't think of any way yet to apply the principles, Dad."

So we talked some more.

I said, "I'll tell you what, if the Savior was right, let's you and I go out in the garage, and I'll make a cat-o-nine-tails whip, and you go over tomorrow and clean out that junior high school of all its iniquities."

"Dad," she said, "you have missed the *point*. You *can't* do that and be popular."

I said, "All right, how's this for an idea? How would it be, the next time you find yourself in that kind of social situation and somebody starts to tell an off-colored story, you stand up and say, 'Now you listen here, we won't have any more of that!' "

She said, "Dad, you just haven't *got* it! I couldn't do *that!*"

Well, I thought maybe she would think that way, and I said, "Well, now, why don't *you* submit a plan?"

She said, "Let me think some more." She walked away with that look, "How did I ever get *you* for a Dad!"

I went about my business. A new day came and went, and as I returned home the next day I found my wife was in the kitchen peeling potatoes for supper. As I approached her to give her a little kiss, I noticed she was holding back the tears. I thought, "Potatoes don't do this."

"What's the matter honey?"

She said, "It is your daughter! Better go see her."

I thought, "Another crisis!" So I tiptoed into the back

bedroom and there was a sweet experience awaiting me. This little lady, who had wrestled with life as it really is, was sitting on the bed pushing back a few tears all of her own, although she is not overly emotional.

I said, "Well, tell me what is the matter."

She said, "Dad, it is an interesting thing. I took the cleansing of the temple story to task today and tried it out."

I said, "Oh, did you clean out the junior high?"

"No," she said, "I called M_____ (who was the girl that had told the off-color story, her LDS friend) and said, 'Can you walk home with me?' 'Yes.' So we walked home. I brought her into the bedroom and sat her down and I said, 'M_____, I just want you to know that our friendship means a great deal to me. Yesterday you really put all of us on the spot. I felt it and I think you did. I know you didn't mean to cause feelings or tension, but when you told that story it reduced all of us in the eyes of our non-Latter-day Saint friends. Now, while I appreciate your intent was maybe honorable and you thought this was a clever way to be noticed, I wonder if the next time you feel that you have to do this would you warn me in advance so that I could be excused?' "

M_____ broke down and put her arms around this daughter and said, "Will you forgive me?"

She said, "Dad, we cried for half an hour." Then the climax: "You know what, Dad?"

I said, "No, what?"

She said, "The New Testament really *works*, doesn't it?"

Yes, "the New Testament really works." Because when you come to understand the concepts and the principles contained in it and you make the proper application in life, it doesn't matter whether you are sitting in a parked car; it doesn't matter whether you are at the ball game; it doesn't matter whether you are in the athletic contest—you will be able to draw upon the gospel principles and solve life's daily challenge and thus find eternal joy and happiness that we each seek.

May I suggest that happiness, as I have come to know it and to appreciate it—limited as it might be—is *being able to discipline self*, to accept the standards of the gospel of Jesus Christ and again make proper application to daily living.

(*BYU Speeches of the Year*, "Happiness Is . . .," April 18, 1967, pp. 6-9.)

**PAUL  H.  DUNN**

## *"He Is a Priesthood Man"*

May I just conclude with one final thought. Just the other day another father told me of a great experience. He said he was sitting in his living room, visiting with his family late Sunday afternoon, when his little eight-year-old son asked him this question: "Daddy, are you going to sacrament meeting tonight?" The father replied, "Yes, son." The son then asked, "Why?"

And while the father contemplated what profound answer he might give to the question, the little seven-year-old sister who was sitting also at the father's knee said very quickly and simply, "Because he is a priesthood man, that's why." The father could not have been more proud.

And may I say tonight, brethren, that more important than being a Princeton man, a Yale man, a Harvard man, or any other kind of man, is the honor of being a "priesthood man." That is the great lesson I have learned tonight again as I have listened to the testimony of President McKay, who has exemplified these very principles in deed.

(*Conference Report*, April 8, 1967, pp. 92-93.)

PAUL H. DUNN

---

## *"Love, Your Home Teacher"*

I would like to share a little experience that happened not too long ago in our home. I have a home teacher whom I wish we could put on a mimeograph and run off for the whole Church. I hope your home teacher has understanding of people and a commitment to the cause like mine. He is not a professional educator. He is a self-made businessman, but he is dedicated and he understands himself and others.

He was assigned to visit our family about three years ago. (I can appreciate that he might have had some concern getting the name of a General Authority. You know, "All the names in the Church and I draw one of these guys!") He called me on the telephone. "Brother Dunn, I have been assigned to be your new home teacher. I am wondering if we could set up a schedule that would be conducive to you and to me."

I said, "Certainly," so we agreed that the following Thursday would be his first visit. We set it for 7:30, giving us time to clear up the dinner dishes and get the family together. At 7:25 on the appointed night, I got the front room ready and turned on the porch light. (I hope you can understand that I am not normally a snoopy person, but I love to study people. I learn a great deal by observing people and their reactions.)

This particular night was no exception; I walked to the dining room window where the curtains were drawn and waited for my home teacher to come. About twenty-five minutes after the hour, a car pulled up, the headlights went out, and I could see that he and his little companion, a fifteen-year-old boy, were having a word of prayer. I know; I have sat in that seat a few times myself. So I bowed my head at the window; I prayed, too, that the Dunns might be receptive, that our visitors might have the courage of their convictions to present their message.

Then he got out of the car. I'll never forget that last moment of getting fresh courage. He walked back and forth on the curb for a minute and then he put his arm around that little companion and up to the door they came.

I quickly backed away from the window and waited for the bell to ring. (You know, you don't want people spying on you.) He rang the doorbell and I waited about thirty seconds before stepping to the door and opening it.

"Good evening, Brother Dunn." He introduced me to his young companion. I escorted them into the front room and went and got my wife and one daughter. Then I made a parental faux pas—*I called* to the daughter who was downstairs. (This tells you a little about home life, I suppose—how we treat one another when we don't understand.) I called downstairs gently "Can you come up, honey? Home teachers are here."

Then came that resounding voice from the basement, "How long is it going to be?" Well, there's real insight there, both ways. I knew that quip would be out all over the Church before long. I went down and brought her upstairs. She asked again on the way, "My favorite program is on. How long is he going to be?"

"We owe it to them," I said. "Let's go in, honey."

The family gathered around, and our home teacher began. He was nervous, I could tell. But because he cared about people, he had taken time to learn a little bit about each one of my family members. He started out with little Kellie. She was about five then. He said, "Kellie, I understand that Miss Finlinson is your kindergarten teacher. Is that right?"

"That's right."

"What is your favorite subject?"

This little gal started to open up and talk. It usually takes her days to get her going the way she did then. But he was right there with her. He asked about Candy and Pam, her little girl friends—because he cared and had taken time to find out about Kellie's particular interests. He could lose himself in others.

He went on to visit with my second daughter. He knew a little about her love life and some of her other interests; he had found a level on which they could communicate.

I remember that he turned then to our oldest daughter, Janet, who is now a student at this very university. He said, "Janet, is your dad holding a family home evening?"

There I was, really on the spot. Under my breath I said, "Come on, honey, answer it right!"

"Yes."

"Is it the kind of an experience that you like?"

"Sometimes."

He looked at me, as though to ask, "Brother Dunn, what are you going to do to make it a good experience all the time?"

Addressing daughter number two, he asked, "Tell me, if your dad could make your family home evenings even better than they are, what would you suggest that he do?"

And do you know what that girl answered? She didn't even pause: "Could you get him to quit talking so much?"

He turned to me, "Did you get the message, Elder?"

I got it. You see, here was a man who understood what he was supposed to do. He understood the program. As they stood and were ready to leave. he asked. "May we kneel in prayer, Brother Dunn?"

"We'd be honored."

So we knelt down and prayed. He left a beautiful spirit in our home. On the way to the door, he asked me, "Brother Dunn, what specifically are you doing to give your family a spiritual experience every week?"

You know, that made me think. "Well, I come home once in a while."

"No," he said, "I mean different than that."

I said, "Well, other than what we try in our little family get-togethers, not too much. We pray together, we have fun together, but I don't know that I am giving them a spiritual experience."

Then he challenged me to read the scriptures to my family and interpret them and have a good experience in this way. Time won't permit further details, but my home teacher followed through and kept me committed until we increased the spirituality in our home—all this, accomplished by a wonderful home teacher who understands people.

To add a quick postscript, one week later—it wasn't in his handbook and the bishop didn't tell him he had to, but because he understood people—this good brother called at our door unannounced.

I answered and was surprised to see him. "What are you doing here tonight? Have I forgotten the night of our appointment?"

"No," he said. "Could I see your daughter Marsha for just a minute?"

"Why, certainly. We are almost ready to sit down to dinner."

I escorted him into the front room and went out into the kitchen where Marsha was setting the table. "Marsha, our home teacher wants to see you."

"What did I do?"

"I don't know. Why don't you go see?"

So she tiptoed in. He wasn't a minute with her. I heard the front door shut as she came into the kitchen, carrying a little box, nicely gift wrapped. It was her birthday and somebody besides the family cared enough to remember! Pleased, she exclaimed, "Look!"

"What is it?" I asked.

"I don't know."

"Why not open it and find out?"

So she set it down, opened it—and there was a beautiful little corsage. The attached card said, "Happy Birthday, Marsha. Been thinking about you all day. Love, Your Home Teacher."

How do you think she responded the next time he called? You see, this is one of the great keys to success in this life, the ability to lose yourself in the lives of others.

---

(*BYU Speeches of the Year*, "Keys To Successful Living," February 13, 1968, pp. 10-14.)

---

PAUL H. DUNN

### *"Death in a Foxhole"*

My mind immediately was called back to a day about twenty years ago when, as a young soldier participating in the activity of this country during World War II, I found myself on the island of Okinawa, somewhere in my nineteenth year. In that serious mortal conflict, while trying to do what we could to preserve these very freedoms that have been discussed today, by chance I fell into the good graces of another young man who had fine ideals and high standards. Almost automatically we got together and shared the experiences of the war together. Frequently we shared the same foxhole. One night during the month of May, our forces had sustained such heavy casualties that it became necessary for my friend and me to be separated. We were in different holes about fifty yards apart. It had commenced to rain about seven that evening, and it was a cold night. Along about eleven the enemy let go with a barrage that was almost unbelievable, and for almost two hours they harassed our lines with heavy artillery and mortar fire. Shortly after midnight one of these shells landed in the hole of my good friend. I could tell from the sound of the blast that it was serious. I called to him but couldn't get an answer, and the type of fighting we did in the Pacific prevented me from crawling over to offer aid. About an hour later I got a faint response indicating life still existed. All that night long, under heavy fire, I tried to call words of comfort to him, and finally as it commenced to get light I crawled to the hole of my friend and found that he had almost become submerged in the water from the heavy rain of the night before.

As I lifted him out on that cold, muddy bank and laid his head in my lap, I tried to offer what physical comfort I could under those conditions, wiping his brow and face with a handkerchief. He was almost limp with death now. I said,

"Harold, you hold on, and I'll get you to the aid station just as soon as I can. It's only a few hundred yards away. "No," he said, "I know this is the end, and I've held on as long as possible because I want you to do two things for me, Paul, if you would." I said, "You just name it, Harold." He said, "If you are permitted to live through this terrible ordeal, will you somehow get word to my parents and tell them how grateful I am for their teaching and influence which has enabled me to meet death with security and calmness, and this in turn will sustain them." And I'm happy to report to you I was able to fulfill that commitment.

"Second, Paul," he said, "if you ever have the opportunity to talk to the youth of the world, will you tell them for me that it is a sacred privilege to lay down my life for the principles that we have been defending here today." And with that testimony on his lips he like so many others before, gave his life for the principles of freedom and righteousness.

Well, as we buried Harold along with his comrades, close friends, and associates, we placed over a cemetary on Okinawa this inscription, and I think it still stands for all to observe who would: "We gave our todays in order that you might have your tomorrows."

---

'*The Improvement Era*, "Who Shall Lead Them?", December, 1965, p. 1147.)

---

### PAUL H. DUNN

### *"Staff Sergeant Isso"*

At the beginning of World War II, Paul H. Dunn, of the First Council of Seventy, was drafted into the United States Army. He was eighteen years of age and had just a few months earlier commenced a very promising professional baseball career. He was sent to the East Coast, and, out of 20,000 men, he was the only Latter-day Saint. He was assigned to Hawaii to undergo general training for a period of time prior to assignment to the South Pacific. The training completed, the men were to have one weekend in Honolulu before shipping out and into combat. Elder Dunn tells the story as follows:

"I had, in this whole procedure of getting involved in that division and finally going over seas, a sergeant I cannot describe. Let me just say that he was the most miserable, unrighteous person I have ever known. . . . He had tremendous power and authority; he could motivate people. . . . He couldn't say three words without profaning two of them. Let's call him Sergeant Isso, to protect identity. Sergeant Isso and Private Dunn had a personal war going on within World War II. . . . When the time came for the pass in Hawaii he lined up his thirty men (he was our platoon leader) and these were pretty good soldiers after a fashion, and he had another philosophy. He called it 'be a man.' . . . Well, here's Isso out there with his thirty men. He says, 'tonight we're going into Honolulu.' And there's a big old two-and-a-half ton truck they backed up. And he said, 'Now men, some of you haven't yet arrived in manhood. You've gone through training; you're pretty good, but we want a symbol in our platoon of being the whole soldier.' And he says, 'it's going to be a tattoo. That's an order. . . . You're not going to come back here tonight without it; and if you do, I'll throw the book at you. I'll give you every detail in the book.' That isn't the way he said it. He was far more descriptive. . . . 'The other thing is that when we get into Honolulu before you're on your own, because some of you haven't conquered woman, you're going to have an experience in a house of prostitution. And that's an order.' And two of us said, 'oh yah?' He said, 'Yah, that's right. . . .'

"I didn't come back with a tattoo or the experience. I got thirty straight days of KP . . . guard duty every night on top of it, because I didn't give in. I woke up one night before we shipped out and found my arm strapped to the bunk and Sergeant Isso, my leader, sitting on my chest with two other fellows holding me down while he attempted to pour a fifth of whiskey into my mouth. He said, 'You're going to qualify, kid.' Well, this went on for two more years, all the way through combat. . . .

. . . At the end of that two years, out of one thousand men in the second battalion, six of us were left alive . . . the others killed, wounded, sent home. Wouldn't you know—Isso and Dunn were two of the six. Well, finally it came time to go home, and we had a point system which was a fair way they thought of locating you home. They gave you one point for each month you served in the service, one extra point for each month overseas, five points for every campaign, five for every time you were shot or wounded. And they posted out scores in Hokaido, Japan, and PFC Dunn had 87 points; Staff Sergeant Isso—85. What a thrilling moment that was. That meant I was going home a whole week ahead of him. And so they gave me a party the night before I was supposed to go. All the gang got together in an old barracks and threw in their cookies and other good things from home. Right in the middle of the party, Isso got up and walked out in the circle and said, 'I want to talk to you, men.' He turned to me and said, 'Paul, I want you to know, and I want this whole group to know that you and I have had a personal battle going on. I don't think Paul does know that I have planned and organized personally every single thing I've tried to get him to do. Do you want to know why?'

" 'I'd like to.'

"He said, 'Because in my own way of life and the activities I have been involved with, I never felt comfortable with you.' And he said, 'The only way I could feel I could be comfortable with you was to put you in the gutter. And you wouldn't let me.' And he said with tears in his eyes as he looked at those other crude characters, 'If I could go home tomorrow to my wife and two kids with his record, morally, I'd give my life. . . .'

"Seven years passed. And one night a knock came at my door. And I answered it. And, lo and behold, there in the framework stood Staff Sergeant Isso. I almost shut the door. I didn't want to invite him in; but I did. He came in, sat down, and said, 'Paul, I've been trying to find you for five years. . . . You know, I wasn't home in Pennsylvania more than six weeks when a knock came at my door. Two of your missionaries came to call. The only reason I let them in was because it was your faith. I'm happy to tell you that another six months later we joined the Church. I wonder, Paul, if you and your wife would do us the honor of coming to the temple tomorrow and being our witnesses. Would you?'

" 'Would I!'

"The next day as I went out to stand in that holy house, watching this sergeant who had been worthless join hands with a beautiful woman and now four children, I saw the gospel of Jesus Christ in action. I saw the most miserable human being this world has ever produced become a living son of the Father."

PAUL H. DUNN

## *"Six Feet Four Inches Tall and a Spirit to Match"*

I had a great athlete who was a member of the Church come take a class from me at the University of Southern California some years ago—big fellow, about six feet four inches and two-hundred and twenty pounds. He was an all-American boy from the physical standpoint. He was at USC on a four-year, fully paid football scholarship. And he had a right; he had earned it. Everybody clamored for him. I think he could have gone to any one of sixty colleges. He had one problem—he thought he was the only thing that existed. And as he walked around the campus he gave that air and authority. The only reason he came to the institute was that I had a class at noon that had twenty-eight girls in it and two boys. That was his motivation.

He used to time his entrance into the class just following the opening prayer, and he would plop down on the back row, put his feet up on an adjoining chair. And then a sneer would come on his face which suggested, "Brother Dunn, I'm here. I dare you to teach me."

Did you ever see a student like that? It is a real challenge to a teacher, I promise you. Try as I would—I put on floor show after floor show for him—I couldn't penetrate his shell. He was just too hard, because he was turned in, selfish. The only time he would look interested was if we were honoring him at some event or banquet.

Talk about discouragement! I would go home and tell my wife, "I'm through. I quit. I can't teach." That would usually be about Thursday or Friday.

And she would grab me by the arm and say, "You can! Go get him!"

By Monday morning I would charge back. "I'm gonna get that boy!"

By Wednesday, down in the valley of despair I'd go. "I can't, I can't!"

"Yes, you can!"

I guess I resigned every week for six weeks.

One day I got a telephone call from a very close friend of mine in Hollywood. He had had a little baby born prematurely, and it wasn't expected to live. They had it in an incubator at the Hollywood Children's Hospital, and he wondered if I could hurry over and help administer to it and give it a name and a blessing before it passed on. I was honored. I hurried over, and in my anxiety to get to the third or fourth floor (I have forgotten which) where the incubators were located, I got off one floor too soon. And, lo and behold, I found myself standing in the orthopedic ward of the Hollywood Children's Hospital—thirty little beds lined up. Have you ever been up to the Primary Children's Hospital to see those little children, confined, many of them with crippled bodies? I don't know what it does to you, but to this dad—it touches him. I was deeply touched.

So, after completing the administration I came back to take a second look at those little children, and again it affected me. This time I noticed they had some volunteers working with them. And so I stepped up to the desk and asked the nurse, "What's going on here?"

She said, "Well, we have a little program where two days a week people from the community come in and try to brighten their day."

"How do you get involved?"

She said, "It is easy, sign right here."

Now I took the pen really wanting to put down my own name, and I couldn't. I was inspired to put my student's name, ol' Bill. So I wrote his name in place of mine.

She said, "Thank you," and called me by his name.

I had signed for the following Thursday, I think it was six o'clock in the evening. I didn't have the heart to go tell him what I had done. You see, he was the type of a person that would have refused had you asked him because we weren't honoring him. To do something for somebody else? "Haven't got time, I'm too busy." So I waited until five o'clock on the following Thursday, which was the date of our appointment. I rang him up on the phone, and his mother answered and I said, "Is Bill there?"

She said, "Yes, we're just ready to sit down to supper."

I said, "May I speak to him for a minute?"

"Certainly."

I learned a long time ago in World War II that the element of surprise is necessary in combat. Bill came to the phone and he said, "Hello?"

And I just reared back and I said, "Bill! Will you help me, please!"

He said, "Oh, yes, sir. Yes, sir. But who is it?"

I said, "It's your institute teacher, Brother Dunn. Thank you, I'll be by and pick you up in fifteen minutes," and I just hung up.

Well, I wish you could have been in the car with me. I drove over and he was standing out on the curb. He had his letterman's sweater on, all three stripes showing, and a half of an apple pie in his hand, eating it. I pulled over to the curb and opened the door and I said, "Get in quick!"

He said, "What's the matter?"

I said, "Get in and I'll tell you."

And he got in, and I slammed the door, and I think he thought we had just received a call to go back to Missouri. Then I just sped off. I sped off, knowing that when I did tell him, he would probably bail out. I got around the corner doing about forty. He said, "What's the excitement?"

I said, "Bill, I really appreciate you."

He said, "For what, for what?"

I said, "You're going down to the Children's Hospital and read to some kids."

He said, "I'm what?" Well, he wouldn't talk to me the rest of the trip.

We got to the hospital. I literally pushed him out on the sidewalk. I gave him a note—third floor and the name of the nurse—and drove off and left him. I had said, "I'll be back in an hour and get you. The Lord bless you."

Well, an hour later I came back, and out of that hospital door walked a new man. He got in the car, and he couldn't talk.

I said, "Well, how'd it go, Bill?"

"I can't tell you."

I said, "I understand. Don't try, but when you get your composure, let me know." So I turned on the car radio so the silence wouldn't be so obvious. We drove for about ten minutes.

Then he turned the radio off. He said, "Brother Dunn, that is one of the great experiences of my life."

I said, "I thought it would be. What happened?"

He said, "They assigned me to a little three-year-old girl that was born without a spine, never known a day out of bed. And that little girl was happier than me. What's the matter with me?" (I wanted to tell him, but that wasn't the place.) And then he went on to say that he was given a chair, and it was brought up to the side of the bed. All the time he was reading she wanted to hold his hand. He read to her out of a giant pop-up Pinnochio book. And he said, "You know, it is embarrassing to read to kids, particularly when people can hear you. But you know, after I finished the first page, I didn't care who heard me."

Then he went on to say he finished the story and then another and another, and finally it was time to go.

He said, "Brother Dunn, I made ready to go, and the little girl didn't want me to. She pulled me down, and you know her whole hand barely fit around one of my fingers. And then she gave me a kiss on the nose and asked me to come back next week. Brother Dunn, you might think I'm a nut, but I signed up for another month."

"No, I don't think you're a nut, Bill. This is what we've been trying to talk about in class. See, you can talk about theories and lesson plans all you want. But you found out what the Lord said, as Luke records it, when you lose yourself in the service of others, you find the real you. This is the greatness of the gospel."

Bill discovered it in his nineteenth year. Two weeks later a knock came at my door, and he filled the whole framework. I said, "What is it, Bill? What can I do to help you?"

"Well," he said, "I've really done it this time."

"What did you do?"

He said, "I just resigned my scholarship—four years!"

"Now, what did you do that for?"

"Just accepted a mission. I'm going out and kind of lose myself."

I spoke at his farewell. Two years later he returned. He blessed me with a little visit. I am proud to announce to you that when Bill came back—he was still six feet four inches tall and two-hundred and twenty pounds—but he had a spirit to match it. What a great contribution he will make to the world—to the Church—because he followed the admonition of the Savior.

---

(*BYU Speeches of the Year*, "Know Thyself—Control Thyself—Give Thyself," October 7, 1969, pp. 13-16.)

# Biographical Sketch

## ELDER ALVIN R. DYER

Elder Alvin R. Dyer was called to be an Assistant to the Council of the Twelve on October 11, 1958. He was ordained an apostle on October 5, 1967. On April 6, 1968, he became a member of the First Presidency and served in that capacity until the death of President David O. McKay on January 18, 1970, after which Elder Dyer resumed a previous position as an Assistant to the Council of Twelve.

Elder Dyer presided over the Central States Mission for four and one-half years followed by two years over the European Mission with headquarters in Frankfurt, Germany. He returned from that assignment in January of 1962.

Elder Dyer was an engineer in the heating and ventilation field, once holding membership in the American Society of Heating and Ventilating Engineers. During World II he served with the American military engineers, acting as a consultant during the early part of the war. At one time he was active with the Exchange Club. During his service as president of the Central States Mission, he became a member of the Missouri Historical Society, a membership he still holds.

Elder Dyer's education, beyond high school, has been obtained largely on a self-teaching basis. He took many correspondence courses to get needed information for his profession. He obtained a journeyman's rating as a sheet metal worker (1925-1933), a trade which assisted him materially in his heating and ventilating profession. He was manager of the heating department of the Utah Builders Supply from 1934 to 1949. At this time he organized his own company which was highly successful, known as the Dyer Distributing Company. In 1955 he disposed of his interest in this company. He has no professional interests at present, devoting all of his time to the Church.

One of thirteen children, Elder Dyer was born January 1, 1903, in Salt Lake City to Alfred Robert and Harriet Walsh Dyer. He married May Elizabeth Jackson in the Salt Lake Temple. The have two children—Gloria May Klein and Brent Rulon—and six grandchildren.

In April 1958 he was called, while still president of the Central States Mission, to be the first assistant general superintendent of the Young Men's Mutual Improvement Association. After seven months he became a General Authority.

Elder Dyer has held many other positions in the Church, extending back to 1924 when he returned from a 26-month mission in the eastern states, where he was the supervising elder of the New York District. He served as the superintendent of the Young Men's Mutual Improvement Association in the sixteenth Ward of the Salt Lake Stake, after which he was called to be the first counselor in the bishopric of the Fifteenth Ward of the same stake, a position held for seven years. He subsequently served for eight years on two stake high councils, seven in the Salt Lake Stake and one in the Riverside Stake. He later served as Sunday School superintendent of the Yalecrest Ward of the Bonneville Stake, and upon division of that ward, he served as second counselor in the bishopric of the Monument Park Ward for three and one-half years and then as bishop for more than five years.

Elder Dyer is the author of many books, some dealing with history, such as *The Refiner's Fire* and *This Age of Confusion*.

His many years of missionary service led to the publication of several books in this area. These are *The Challenge, The Meaning of Truth,* and *The Lord Speaketh.* Other books are *The Fallacy* and, most recent, *Who Am I?.* The latter deals with the meaning of life and man's destiny.

Athletically minded, Elder Dyer played high school baseball and M Men basketball and at one time bowled in major league circles. Of late he plays handball. At one time, following his first mission, he had an opportunity to play professional baseball, but the offer was declined because of Church responsibilities.

# ALVIN R. DYER

## *"Would You Like to Know More?"*

You know, there are many of the Church leaders now that are traveling every week by air to go to the various stakes of the Church, and occasionally we travel with some of the women of the general boards, which is not often the case. But sometimes when a reorganization is needed, we have to inject our service in on their program.

Such was the case recently when Brother LeGrand Richards and I were assigned to go to the South Carolina area, there to divide that stake, creating a new stake. We had one of the representatives of the Relief Society and of the Primary with us on the plane.

I saw to it that they were comfortably seated in two of the three seats that are on each side of these jet planes. They call it an economy jet. As I left them to go up toward the front of the plane to sit with Brother Richards, I said to myself, "I wonder which one of these sisters will ask that man by the window the question." Because, you know, this is on our minds, and the golden questions, "What do you know about the Mormon Church?" and "Would you like to know more?" have become legendary, and everybody seeks for the opportunity to ask them.

I turned around and I saw them whispering to each other, and I thought they were deciding it. Finally, one of them broached the subject about how smooth the plane was flying at 29,000 feet and got into a conversation, and then finally got the courage to say to this man, "What do you know about the Mormon Church?" (They had explained that they were going down to South Carolina to hold a conference.)

"Well," he said, "I know quite a bit about the Mormon Church."

She immediately said, "Would you like to know more?"

He said, "I sure would. I need all the help I can get. You see, I'm a stake president."

(*BYU Speeches of the Year*, "Stand Up and Be Counted," March 20, 1963. p. 2.)

ALVIN R. DYER

## *"Dad Wants You to Come Back"*

I bear you my testimony in all humility that this is the work of God. I have seen it in the lives of people. I have witnessed it as it causes men and women to change their lives. I have seen it become a motivating force for good, and I bear record that Jesus Christ is the Son of God, the Redeemer of the world, the Mediator—not as it is preached by these predominant countries of the lands of Europe. And do you know that this is the message we declare when we go to the doors of the people for the first time? It is through the testimony of our missionaries that the veneer of false concepts and the antiquities of these people are being laid aside for the acceptance of the gospel. It is more powerful than all other things that we do in our missionary work as we look into their faces and bear record that God has raised up a prophet, and they are listening to this message.

We had a family of seven visited recently by the missionaries where the woman was about to close the door when the elder said, "I can see you are going to close the door. I am very sorry. We have such a wonderful message." And we have told them, "Before any door is closed, you bear your testimony." He said, "Before you close that door, I want to bear my testimony to you of these brief things we have stated today," and he bore his testimony. The door closed, and the missionaries started for their home when they heard a voice. It was the young boy of the home, fourteen-years-old, who said, "Dad wants you to come back." And they went back, and the father said, "I listened to your message at the door on the other side as you spoke to my wife, and I did not think much of it until that young man bore his testimony. And then something came over me that I have never experienced before, and now I have to know what this is."

I had the privilege of shaking hands with this family of seven and hearing them testify that God had made known to them that these things are true. This is the reason why so many are accepting the gospel in the lands of Europe. We are proclaiming the message by testimony and through the Spirit.

(*Conference Report*, October 8, 1960, p. 62.)

ALVIN R. DYER

## "The Font Is Filled"

These new converts are telling their neighbors about the gospel. They are letting their friends know about it. Let me tell you of one typical case. When I was in Denmark, I shook hands with a good sister by the name of Dagmar Petersen, who had been baptized a month previously. She had heard the gospel, but she said, "I am too old. All of my family would turn against me. I know Joseph Smith is a prophet of God, but I do not think I'd better take the step."

But thank the Lord for a missionary who had the courage to go to her one day when there was a baptismal service and say to her, "Sister Petersen, today is the day of your baptism: The font is filled. Will you come with me?" She hesitated for a moment, then went with the missionaries, walking the six or seven blocks to our beautiful little chapel, and was there baptized.

In this conference meeting she sat with one neighbor on one side and two neighbors on the other side of her. The one on the one side already had been baptized, and the other two were to be baptized the following Saturday. And she said, "I will never be happy until all my friends and all my neighbors have been baptized." And this wonderful soul left the chapel and then came back. She said, after entering the chapel again, "I cannot leave, the spirit is so great in this building. I must shake hands again," and then she went off down the street with her friends.

(*Conference Report*, October 8 1960, p. 60.)

ALVIN R. DYER

## *"The Mayor of Reykjavik"*

I recall a fulfillment in this type of procedure when in London, England, in the early part of 1961

with President McKay. He had gone there to dedicate the Hyde
Park Chapel and to place a plaque on the front of the little
Wales residence at Merthyr Tydfil, the birthplace of his mother.
He said to me, "President Dyer, I want you to go to Iceland
to investigate the possibilities of sending missionaries there."

Through obedience to his request, within a few weeks
we had taken an Icelandic Airways plane from Oslo, Norway,
in company with the president of the Norwegian Mission, and a
legal representative of our Church who was then in Europe,
and my son, who was serving then in the European Mission
office. As we flew to Iceland we had the thrilling experience,
out over the Arctic Ocean, of having one of the motors on the
plane go out in mid-air. This is always a very pleasant experience—to look out the window and see the propeller standing
still. But the pilot said, "Don't worry about it; it has been
'feathered,'" which means that the propeller blade is adjusted
to knife the stream of air and not against the air. So he said,
"We will successfully land at Reykjavik." This we did, but I
noticed they had all the crash equipment ready, so he was not
so sure.

But what do you do when you go to a country like this,
to establish an image for the Church? In the few days that we
were there we decided upon a procedure which, I think, is a
good one. First we visited the embassy of the United States,
which is always a protective measure to follow when you are
away from home. One thing happened there that impressed me
very much.

After we got through with our business wherein we inquired
about the customs of the people, of religious tolerations and
restrictions, and other things that obtained in Iceland that
could affect the sending of missionaries there, the ambassador
said, "Are all Latter-day Saints like Barney Timmins?"

I said, "Why do you ask?" Fortunately, I happened to know
of him, but I did not know that he had been there.

He said, "He was attached to our embassy here for a
number of years, and if all Latter-day Saints are like that young
man, then you must have a wonderful church."

I thought of the influence for good that an individual can

leave in a place and how he can lift the image of the Church when he stands on the things that he believes in and obeys the standards that he has been taught.

We left the office of the ambassador and went to the office of the head bishop of the Luthern Church on the island, where we had a very pleasant visit and heard the bishop speak of his high regard for this young man, a Latter-day Saint—Barney Timmins.

From there we went to the office of the minister of education. At each of the places of contact, we spoke of our purpose in going there, always with the idea we had been asked to come by the president of our Church, whom we feel is a prophet of God. "What would you think of missionaries being sent to the island of Iceland?" we asked, and explained what the missionaries did.

Every contact that we made evidenced a truly sincere welcome. We were privileged to meet with the president of the University of Iceland. This is always, I think, an especially good contact to make. We talked to him about the Brigham Young University and the educational program of the Church, the desire of our people to seek education.

In the course of our discussions, I even suggested that it might be possible that some scholarships could be arranged for some of the students of the University of Iceland to come to the Brigham Young University in the event that we had missionaries come to their island, so that such young men and women could attend our Church school and then go back to Iceland and become a part of the disseminating of information about the Church.

We finally ended up in the office of the mayor of Reykjavik. His name is Halgrimmson.

I have been greeted and welcomed in many places throughout the world in a very cordial manner, but never so much as here this day in the office of Mayor Halgrimmson. When I suggested that we might send missionaries there, if it was the will of the presidency and the presiding brethren of the Church, he said, "For me, I would like to see the Mormon missionaries here right now." He said, "What will you do with them when they come? Where will they live?"

I said, "They will find a place with the people."

He said, "Now I want this to be my responsibility. When they come, I will see to it that they have a place to live. Where will you hold your meetings?"

"Well, this is a little premature. We only have two members of the Church in Iceland—a Danish woman and her son."

He said, "You will need some place to meet. Let it be the responsibility of the city of Reykjavik to provide you with a meeting place at no cost."

I said, "Mayor Halgrimmson, you have been very friendly, and kind, and I would like to know the reason. Why are you so friendly to the Mormon Church?"

"Well," he said, "the answer is simple. Some years ago two Mormon missionaries came to the island of Iceland and they learned that many of the Icelanders left the island to go to Westmanna Island, some 150 kilometers off the coast of Iceland, toward the Arctic Circle. There, employed by others in one of the great fishing areas of the world, they would fish. So these missionaries, I suppose being fishermen at heart, got on a boat and away they went to Westmanna Island. While the men fished in the day, they fished at night and baptized 150 of these fishermen. They came back to the island and later, with their wives and families who were also converted, many of them emigrated to America. A good number of them, as many of you know, settled in Springville and Spanish Fork."

As he continued this story he said, "My uncle was among them. Last year (which would have been in the fall of 1960) my wife and I decided to come to America. We did not come in any official capacity, as the mayor of Reykjavik and his wife, but just as ordinary Icelanders. We told no one of our coming. We bought an automobile in Detroit, and toured America. We went of course to Utah, where we spent three weeks—three of the most wonderful weeks of my life. You ask me why I would like to see missionaries in Iceland. I lived among your people for those three weeks. I came to know them. I have never been so impressed with people, their educational inclinations, their industry, and, above all, their desire to abide by what they believe and what they were taught.

"We went to Salt Lake City for the last few days of our visit in Utah. We stayed in a motel near the temple. The manager of that motel was the kindest, perhaps the finest man I have ever met. He said he belonged to some kind of quorum, but this was a man who lived completely, in my estimation, the life of a Christian."

I thought then and there of the tremendous influence that we as a people, both individually and as a community, can wield upon the lives of other people if only we live the gospel. I think that when the time comes to open Iceland for the preaching of the gospel—and this is bound to come—probably this one man with the influence he wielded on Mayor Halgrimmson and his wife will be largely responsible for the opening of the doors of preaching the gospel in Iceland. I have not been able to find this brother as yet, and I have been looking for him, but when I do I will want to convey this glad news to him.

These are happenings that indicate how the spirit of God works in the minds of people to open the way for the spreading of the gospel.

*(BYU Speeches of the Year, "Stand Up and Be Counted", March 20, 1963, p. 3-6.)*

# ALVIN R. DYER

## *"Elder Kahne"*

But there is one experience that came out of this that I want to mention this morning. As we traveled through the city we came to a certain area, and Dr. Novinski stopped the government car in the midst of a number of very wonderful buildings that had been recently constructed.

These buildings were not ordinary structures. They were well built, indicating that the Polish people must have sacrificed other building needs to provide the materials for these, for there is a shortage of materials in Warsaw and in Poland. Dr. Novinski then explained that we were standing in the area once known as the Warsaw Ghetto—that infamous place to which the Jewish people of Europe were shipped from the conquered countries, there to await their eventual deportation to the exterminating chambers, which were not very far away.

As I stood there thinking of what the Polish people had done in erasing or endeavoring to erase from their memory the terrible experience of this place and the terrible inhumanities that had been brought upon the Jewish people, I thought of the experience of one of our young missionaries then serving in France who was in this ghetto with his mother and father. He is a Belgian Jew. The time had come for them to be taken to the gas chambers. He came out with his hand in his father's hand, but somehow, in some way that he is not able to explain, from his written testimony to me, he was taken by the hand by someone else and was not led to the truck that awaited them to take them to the gas chamber. Instead, in some way he was led out of the camp. How this was accomplished he does not even know. Maybe it was because he was too young and was not fully aware of what was transpiring. At any rate, he remained secreted in the environs of Warsaw and was not found.

After the war he returned to Belgium. His father and mother, of course, had both been exterminated that day. His foster father, who had given him a home, knowing his parents, endeavored to do everything for him, to give him the finest education that anyone could have. He was taught French. He was taught English. He was taught German. Because of the brilliance of his mind he became, I suppose, one of the finest young men that we have ever had in the Church with regards to the French language. But beforehand he was visited by the missionaries as he reached some age of maturity. He told me that he knew the first day that he heard the missionaries testify of the truth of the gospel of Jesus Christ that this was to be his way of life. He was baptized shortly thereafter, although his foster father, a very kind and wonderful man, was not able to receive of the message. Elder Kahne was later called to be a missionary in the French mission, and today (if he has not been released, and at last word he had not been) he is one of our very excellent French translators, having just completed the translation of the Book of Mormon in French, and many other important manuals.

This is an indication to me of the preservation of this man's life for a purpose, and we found this to be true in the calling of many translators in Europe.

(*BYU Speeches of the Year,* "The Gospel of Jesus Christ Is Not Theory," May 9, 1962, pp. 5-6.)

## ALVIN R. DYER

### *"Why These Are Our Teachings!"*

I am thinking of Immo Luschin Ebengreuth of Graz, Austria, a man who heard the gospel message from two missionaries and said to them before they got into a lengthy discussion on the gospel, "I would ask you only five questions before you go further." He was a confirmed member of the Catholic Church, and these are his questions:

1.  "Does this church believe in marriage for all eternity?
2.  "Does this church believe in the punishment for infants who are not baptized?
3.  "Do, in this church, the rich and the poor have equal opportunity?
4.  "In this church, do you baptize by immersion for the remission of sin?
5.  "In this church do you lay on hands for the receiving of the Holy Ghost?"

This man had never met the missionaries before, and we inquired as to where he got such questions. His answer was, "We have not been satisfied with our faith. My wife and I determined that through prayer and the desire to know that we would find out the true church." The missionaries said, "Why, these are our teachings," and thus Brother Ebengreuth was baptized with his wife. This brother is a skilled interpreter. He speaks English, I am confident, better than I do, and he now will become a translator for the Church of the German language.

---

(*Conference Report,* October 8, 1960, p. 60-61.)

# Biographical Sketch

## ELDER MARION D. HANKS

Elder Marion D. Hanks, a General Authority of The Church of Jesus Christ of Latter-day Saints, was named an Assistant to the Council of the Twelve in April, 1968. Formerly he was a member of the First Council of Seventy.

Elder Hanks has been prominent in civic affairs, particularly in the field of youth development. In 1957 he was appointed a member of the United States President's Citizens Advisory Committee on Youth Fitness, on which he served for several years. In this capacity he has spoken at youth conferences throughout the United States and in foreign countries and was a featured speaker at the White House Conference on Children and Youth.

Among his civic services, Elder Hanks was the first chairman of the Utah Committee on Children and Youth, a board member of the national "Operation Fitness" program, member of the boards of Weber College and of the College of Southern Utah. He now serves on the board of trustees of Brigham Young University and is a member of the National Council, Boy Scouts of America.

He has been for many years a teacher and served for a number of years in the leadership of Temple Square. As a young man he filled a two-year proselyting mission for the Church in the northern United States. Recently he and his family spent several years in England and Europe in mission leadership there. Currently Elder Hanks serves as supervisor of the Eastern American Missions, which include the Canadian, Eastern Atlantic States, Eastern States, Cumorah, and New England Missions.

Born in Salt Lake City into a family of seven children, he was two years old when his father died. He was reared by his widowed mother. He attended the public schools and holds a Juris Doctor degree from the law school of the University of Utah. Formerly active in college and other amateur athletics, he is a handball and squash player.

During World War II Elder Hanks served aboard a submarine chaser in the Pacific. In recent years he has visited servicemen at their bases in many parts of the world. He has recently returned from his latest tour of military installations in Vietnam, Thailand, and Hong Kong and also spent time in Israel, Jordan, and Egypt.

Elder Hanks married Maxine Christensen in the Hawaiian Temple, and they are the parents of four daughters and one son.

# MARION D. HANKS

---

## "Look, You Can't Do This to Me"

At the high school I attended, they gave a medal and a watch to one student who qualified in various fields of activity—scholarship, athletics, leadership, etc. I learned a few days before graduation that I was a candidate for this honor. This pleased me, of course. I was especially concerned, therefore—knowing that I had a chance and knowing some fine people who also were candidates and whom I regarded highly—with the marks I got as I went from class to class on that last day. There was not anything to be done now about activities or leadership, but these marks I knew would be significant. So as they came and were satisfactory, I felt good and encouraged, until I got to the last class, which was taught by a marvelous little soul who had taught my oldest brother seventeen years before and all of the family members in between—I was the last.

Because this was a class in English literature, a field in which I had been particularly interested in boyhood, and because I had read most of the materials that were assigned for the class, I did not do very much in terms of contribution. I showed up occasionally, but I found many reasons to be away on athletic or newspaper or studentbody business. When the tests came, I passed them all—got good marks. I had A's down through the year and so I had no feeling that anything else would be forthcoming. But when the report card came back, it had a big fat E on it. Well, I sat shocked and stunned, and then laughed nervously and felt sure that she was playing a little joke on me.

When the class was over and people were showing each other their marks—and I was holding mine back—I found my way to her desk and said, "Look, Miss Young, (again laughing nervously) this is *my* report card. You made a mistake!"

"Oh," she said, "I know that it is your report card, and in fact I have made a mistake, but it was a deliberate one—I wanted you to think a little. I am not going to fail you in the class; that would put your graduation in jeopardy." She took the report card away from me and superimposed a big C over it.

I said, "Look, you can't do this to me."

"Oh, yes I can."

I said, "No, no, open your book." She opened it and we went across the page.

"Look at the marks—ninety, this and this—and compare them with the people you gave the A's to. My marks are better all the way. You can't do this."

She said, "Oh, yes I can. I am going to do it." I asked, "Do you know what this will do to me?"

She answered, "Yes, I know. Let me tell you something. I taught your oldest brother, and I have taught all the ones in between. When I knew you were coming, I was grateful that I would have the last of the Hanks tribe because I loved every one of them, and I wanted to love you. But you made it very hard. Do you think that I am stupid? Don't you think I knew what has been going on? Don't you think I know the excuses you have made and the unmanly way you have acted in this course? Oh, you made the grades all right. You had read most of the material before; I knew that. But you haven't been fair with me or yourself. I am not going to mark you this month on what you did in comparison with anybody else. I am going to mark you in comparison with what you should have done—and you get the 'C'."

I said again, "Do you know what this is going to do to me?" By now I was pretty close to tears—this seemed so unfair.

She said, "Yes, I know, and I would like you to know that I have been up most of the night thinking about it and that I love you too much not to do it."

"C"—and out I went. Well, I didn't get the medal or the watch. My name is not on the plaque. Another fellow's is, a fellow who came down here and became student body president at the BYU. He is a great and good man who deserved it, a better man than I was. But I lived long enough to stand in front of a group of elderly ladies, of which she was one, and tell them and her to her face that this was the most important lesson that I learned in school. *There is not anything in this world worth having that you can get without working for it, without putting out, doing your best.* Before God and wise men we are not going to be judged by what other people do, but by what we do with what we have.

---

(*BYU Speeches of the Year*, "Spiritual Constants In Our Changing Times", January 4, 1961, pp. 5-7.)  ☉

---

**MARION  D.  HANKS**

---

## *"Ah, Let Him Go, He Is Just One Kid!"*

Could I tell you one story which bears repetition—and I have had the blessing of repeating it in some of the stakes of the Church. It is the most significant single experience I have ever had, personally, about the importance of one. It happened long enough ago that I think the individual involved would not be conscious of our noting him, though I see no harm if he is.

A man walked into these grounds and into an office in the Bureau of Information one day long ago. He interrupted a conversation which was private and serious, and did it without apology. He was quite an elderly man; he was not what you would call an attractive human being. He was unkempt, unshaven; he reeked of alcohol and tobacco.

He walked over to the desk where I sat, pointed his hand in the direction of the temple, and said, "How do you get in there?" I assumed that he was a tourist, one of the infrequent but occasional few who do not understand the purpose and the reason of temple-going and who have become affronted because they are not taken into the temple, and perhaps had come to complain.

I told him as best I could, or began to, the story of the temple, but had proceeded only a little distance when he interrupted. He waved me away and said, "Oh, you don't have to tell me all that. I know that. I am a Mormon."

"Well," I said, "if you are a member of the Church and you know all of this, what is it you want from me?" He said, "Frankly, nothing. There isn't anything you have to give me. I am here because my wife insisted on my coming in, but I have fulfilled my errand," and out he went.

I tried to pick up the threads of the conversation and finish it, and later, as I sat thinking about him and his story, I looked out the window and saw him walking by the Joseph and Hyrum [Smith] monuments with a younger woman. I went out to talk with them. She identified herself as his wife. He had been married three times; each previous wife had died after bearing a large family.

There are two questions I asked him, which I think each person here would do well to hear answered as he answered them. I asked, in effect, how he had come to his feelings of antagonism and indifference. He told me that at age nineteen he had been ejected from a chapel by a bishop's counselor who had been summoned because of the boy's troublemaking in class. One thing that had been said this man remembered for nearly sixty years. As he was thrown out, someone objected. The answer that came from the counselor who had the task in hand was, "Ah, let him go, he is just one kid!"

He went, and he never came back, nor was there ever any visiting, never any outpouring or increase of the love that should follow reproof, according to the Lord. He moved to another area of the land, married, had a family; his wife passed away and he married again; his second wife died after bearing a family also. He had come to Salt Lake City at the insistence of his third wife, who, having been taught by the missionaries and converted to the principles of the gospel, had brought him here hoping that somehow he might be touched—he, the member.

This, also, I would like to report: I asked him how many living descendants he had. He counted them and answered, "Fifty-four." I asked him then, how many of them are members of the Church, and I expect you know the answer, though perhaps not his interesting expression. He said, "Huh, ain't any of them members of the Church. They're a pretty hard lot."

This last question: who was it the bishop's counselor propelled out the door that morning? Just one boy? Just one? This one has in his own lifetime become, in effect, a multitude, and the current has but begun to run, and everyone of them denied, according to his own witness, the love of the gospel and the brotherhood of the Saints, the warmth and strength and direction of the programs of the Church.

---

(*Improvement Era*, "Just One Boy," December 1959, pp. 926-927.)

---

## MARION D. HANKS

### *"The Courage of Sergeant 'Red' Irwin"*

The first great B-29 strike on those who were then our enemy, flown from a land base, was led by an airplane named "City of Los Angeles." (There had been previous strikes from carriers, but this was our first flown from our own airfields recovered from the enemy. It was meant to inform him that the war was now to be carried to his own homeland, and it was a very important mission.) Aboard the aircraft were twelve men, eleven regular crewmen and a colonel flying as squadron commander for the mission. They were to reach a rendezvous point fifty to seventy-five miles off the mainland of the enemy, then assume regular fighting formation and fly in on target, which was a complex of high octane gasoline plants feeding the enemy war potential.

Rendezvous point was reached as scheduled, and Colonel Sprouse ordered the dropping of the phosphorous bomb which was to mark the point. Sergeant "Red" Irwin skidded the bomb down the chute as ordered. The act was loaded with death. The flap at the end of the bomb chute had somehow become stuck. When the bomb struck it, it exploded prematurely and burst back into the cabin of the airplane and into the face and chest of Sergeant Irwin. Dropping to the deck it began swifly to burn its way through the thin metal flooring separating it from the incendiary bombs stored in the bomb bay below. In moments the "City of Los Angeles" and its crew would be blown to bits far out over the ocean in enemy territory.

Sergeant Irwin, tragically wounded, got to his knees, picked up the bomb in his bare hands, cradled it in his arms, and staggered up the passageway. Crashing into the navigator's table, he had to stop and unlatch it with fingers that left burn marks in the hardwood. By now the aircraft was filled with acrid fumes blinding the pilot, and was wallowing less than three hundred feet above the water. Irwin staggered into the pilot's compartment shouting, "Window, window." He could not see that it was already open, and his fumbling fingers left burn marks on the metal. He threw the bomb out of the window and collapsed to the deck. Two hours later, Colonel Sprouse having ordered the "City of Los Angeles" back to base in the slim hope that Irwin's life might be saved, they reached Iwo Jima. Irwin's flesh was still smoking with imbedded phosophorous when he was removed from the plane by comrades who had to avert their faces from his tragic wounds.

Sergeant Irwin lived to receive his nation's highest honor for extreme bravery and to survive nearly fifty plastic surgery operations which restored him to a somewhat normal life. He lived to marry and to become a father. And with him there lived eleven other men who but for his almost unbelievable courage would be dead. Eleven men, spared to their lives and work and families through the decision and courageous act of one man! When Sergeant Irwin picked up that bomb, he knew that it was burning at 1,300 degrees Fahrenheit, 1,088 degrees hotter than boiling water!

(*Improvement Era*, "Substance or Shadow," December 1962, pp. 948-49.)

### MARION D. HANKS

## "A Sacred Experience"

May I share a really choice, sacred, personal experience? I was in the missionary home in Salt Lake City, trying to help new missionaries get a sense of their great Christian responsibility, when I had a kind of little vision of my own.

There was a foundation to the vision. The night before in the Salt Lake Tabernacle a man had died of a heart attack while he listened to the choir. He was sitting next to his wife (you could not contrive a situation more emotionally charged) and turned to her as the choir practiced and said, "Martha, after all these years, imagine, we can be here while the choir practices. You know, I don't have to die to go to heaven to hear the angels. This is enough for me." He then sat so quietly that she respected his worshipful attention. But after the rehearsal, when all of the others were stirring and moving and she turned to him, he still didn't move—he had died there on that seat in the tabernacle.

Well, I was called, and that night I made a call. I found out that this lady—a crippled person who was quite elderly and walking with a cane—had come with her husband from Los Angeles in fulfillment of a dream. That night—alone and stricken with this tragic thing—she found a place to stay with a considerate choir member, and I tried to do what I could to be helpful. I found the schedules for her and helped her arrange a train departure and the carrying home of the body. Then I went about my day's activities.

The next day I was in the missionary home at four o'clock, talking to missionaries, as I have said. As I looked at my watch, I had this little vision—the vision of Mrs. Bernarfa, walking by the railing down the ramp at the railroad station, while along came a wagon with a box on it. I had a picture of her, all alone. So I said to the missionaries, "I am sorry, I must go. And I have to go *now*. God bless you. Work hard. Be happy." I ran out the door, got in my car, raced down to the Union Pacific station, left my car where I should not have left it, jumped over a railing, ran down the ramp and there saw the picture I had seen before. I saw this elderly woman with a package on one arm and a cane in her hand. Just then the wagon rolled by with the body of her beloved in a box. I took her by the arm and walked with her to her car, took her to her place in the train, expressed my love and sympathy (which is all that could be done), and went my way.

Let me tell you that this was one of the greatest blessings

of my life, not simply because of the happy things that followed, even though many did. A great pastor down there, for instance, with a wonderful congregation, one of the greatest preachers in the United States, wrote me a letter and said, "I have never had anything good to say about the Mormons before, but I want you to know after what you did for Mrs. Bernarfa that I will never have anything but good to say about you and your people."

That is a little thing—I almost am uneasy saying it— or is it? The satisfactions and the sweet sense of relationship I felt at that moment when I did a little something for somebody were more important than any medal anybody ever pinned on me, any name on a plaque they ever put on the wall, or anything that has been said.

Let me tell you in all sobriety that if you would like to make it a happy day—a good day—get your mind off yourself. Look around you. At the moment of depression, if you will follow a simple program, you will get out of it. Get on your knees and get the help of God; then get up and go find somebody who needs something that you can help them find. Then it will be a good day.

---

(*BYU Speeches of the Year*, "Make It a Good Day!", September 27, 1966. pp. 6-7.)

---

## MARION D. HANKS

### *"Kneel Down, Son"*

Let me give you an example. I sat at a stake conference where a returned missionary bore his testimony. He had but a short time and he chose to use one idea. He thanked God for a great, humble mother, and gave his reason. He said that as a high school boy, he had been sorely tried by the illness and then death of his little sister whom he had loved greatly and who had been the darling of the family, being the last of them. Their father had died. The little girl grew ill, and in spite of prayers and administrations and fasting and much concern, worsened and died in the night. The boy went into his room, locked the door, and sobbed out his broken heart to the walls because he was not willing to do it to the God whom he could not now honestly approach. In his rebellion and anger at a God, if there were one who would permit such a thing to happen to them, he cried out in rebellion. He said he would never pray again, would never go to church again, and could never have any confidence again in a God who would permit this to happen. And in his immature but sincere sorrow, he made some rather serious covenants with himself. He stayed awake the rest of the night, apprehensive about an experience he anticipated. It was their custom, as it is in so many, though not enough, Latter-day Saint homes, to kneel morning and evening with the children around the mother, to thank God for the goodness of his blessings.

He waited for that moment, knowing what he had to say, but fearing it. When his mother said, "Come, children," he said, "No."

She said, "Kneel down, son."

He said, "No, I will not kneel down, and I will never kneel down again."

She said, as I remember his words, and I was deeply touched as were we all. "Son, you're the oldest child in this home. You are the only man in the house, and if I ever needed a man, I need one now. You kneel down."

He knelt down, still rebellious, but because his mother, the idol of his heart, needed him; and he began for the first time to think in terms of her broken heart and her sorrow. So he knelt, but he said to himself, "I wonder what she's going to thank God for this morning." And his mother, knowing as she must have, the questions in his mind and the minds of the other children, taught them the gospel on their knees that morning. She thanked God for what the family knew, for the blessing of eternal ties, for direction and purpose and guidance and convictions as to the future. She thanked God that they had been blessed with this wonderful, angelic child who had brought so much to them and who was to be theirs, always. And out of her mother's heart, knowing the desperate, critical nature of the moment, taught her own children what there was to thank God for under conditions of such stress.

As the boy stood, a successful, dedicated Latter-day Saint who had filled an honorable, difficult mission, he thanked God for a mother who was a heroine, who had the qualities of heroism in every conceivable degree, who represented as marvelous and impressive an example of heroism as I can think of.

(*BYU Speeches of the Year*, "Heroism," 1958-59, pp. 3, 4.)

## MARION D. HANKS

### *"Boy, We Really Have a Swell Bathroom, Haven't We?"*

He who believes knows that he belongs. But he also needs to feel himself an important and accepted part of a group. Young people want and deserve parents and a family they can be proud of. Their capacity to become worthwhile persons is strongly affected by the absence or presence of such a family and by their own acceptance of the challenge to be a contributing, responsible member of it. The influence of a good family is well-captured by this account from an unknown source:

"It was a gorgeous October day. My husband Art and I

were down at the boat landing helping our friend Don drag his skiff up on the beach. Art remarked wistfully that it would be a long time before next summer, when we could all start sailing again. 'You folks ought to take up skiing like our family and have fun the year round.' Don said.

" 'Doesn't that get pretty expensive?' I asked.

"Don straightened up and smiled. 'It's funny,' he said. 'We live in an old-fashioned house—legs on the tub, that sort of thing. For years we've been saving up to have the bathroom done over. But every winter we take the money out of the bank and go on a couple of family skiing trips. Our oldest boy is in the army now, and he often mentions in his letters what a great time we had on those trips. You know, I can't imagine his writing home, "Boy, we really have a swell bathroom, haven't we?" ' "

(*Conference Report*, April, 1969, p. 57.)

## MARION D. HANKS

### *"Say, Hanks, Do You Believe in Jesus Christ?"*

The Christmas story that I want to mention occurred in the middle of the summer some years ago, at a naval training center. The man opposite me in the room had the many stripes on his arm that signified long and distinguished service; I was an apprentice seaman in boot camp. Nonetheless, Commander Hamilton, as he greeted me at the door, was most gracious—called me "Mr. Hanks," seated me with cordiality, and we talked as equals. He had invited me to discuss the possibility of a chaplaincy. I was quick to tell him that because of a mission, I had not finished an academic degree and didn't qualify under the Navy's standards. He as quickly responded that he felt he could do something about getting that requirement waived, all things else being favorable. After a little more conversation, this rangy, fine looking man, who had been over the bow of the Yorktown on a line when she was sunk shortly before, who had everything about him that was manly and attractive to a man and was a chaplain and servant of the Lord, not of our faith, said to me, "Before I recommend you to the Chief of Chaplains, do me a favor, please. Talk to me about your experience in your Church, about what you think may help me recommend you as qualified to represent the Lord in the military chaplaincy."

And so I began, and, I want to protest, with earnestness and honesty, to try to tell him what I felt, out of our common experience in the Church, might qualify me to serve in that very significant role. He who had been so courteous and so kind began to be fidgety, and I quickly knew, as we do when we seek to communicate person-to-person, that I wasn't making it, that I was losing. And I became a little more anxious, trying to tell him what there is, this stage-by-stage opportunity in the Church for a young person to develop the quality to be a servant of God. I told him from the beginning—the early two and a half minute talks, the scouting, the deacon opportunity, the Sunday School teaching, and the mission.

After a time his demeanor completely changed. He finally interrupted me. He said, "Say, Hanks, do you believe in Jesus Christ?"

I said, "Yes, sir. Everything I believe relates to Jesus Christ. The name of the Church that I belong to is his name. My faith revolves around him as my Savior."

He, looking at his watch, said, "Well, you have been talking seven minutes and you haven't said so." I think I have not made that mistake again.

(*BYU Speeches of the Year*, "Was He Relevant?", December 17, 1968, pp. 2-3.)

MARION D. HANKS

---

## *"I Won't Stand Between You and God"*

Once, long ago—so long ago that I would hope and pray no one could identify anyone involved— I went to a hospital in the middle of the night, called by a dearly loved friend of former years. I hadn't seen him for a long time. There had been an accident involving a member of his family who was dying. My friend called me to the hospital, sure that if I arrived something would happen that would help. When I got there, the person was in the operating room, doctors and nurses around him. He was dying, literally.

I sensed that my friend was not with me.

He said, "I'm not going in."

I said, "You can't be serious. Come on."

He said, "I can't go."

I said, "Look, I don't know what you're talking about, but come with me. This is *your* loved one."

He said, "I won't stand between you and God, and I'm not worthy to go in there."

I said, "Look, my friend, if being worthy means to be perfect, or free from sins or problems or bad memories, I can't go either, but that isn't the way it is! God has given us the commission and the authority. Come on!"

He said, "I won't go."

So I went alone. And before I could begin the administration, his loved one was gone.

I won't repeat the detail that followed, what he said. But I'd like you to put yourself in that position. Can you be that personal? The time will come, maybe not just that way, but I promise you in the name of the Lord, it will come, when you will have a chance either to lend the strength of your faith or to be unwilling to participate.

Oh, God bless you, as I earnestly pray He'll bless me, with

sense enough to know that at the *banquet of consequences*, when we go with our loved ones, there will not be much that is satisfying at the table unless I am able to bow my head, not hang it, in the presence of God who will be there.

---

(*BYU Speeches of the Year*, "The Banquet of Consequences," October 3, 1967, pp. 11-12.

---

## MARION D. HANKS

### *"Gerry"*

Let me give you a headline of an experience not unfamiliar to many of you. Some of you have made a different answer already I suppose. A fine girl whom we'll call Gerry, which wasn't her name, was invited by her other high school associates, she being a freshman, to attend a social which was to be the year's introduction of the freshmen girls of high social level to this particular group. Gerry went, thrilled. She had a natural desire to be appreciated and popular; she wanted to succeed. Her mother was equally pleased because the girls who had invited her were fine girls so far as she knew. She had a new dress, was all pretty and ready when they called. She went to the place and found that she, after a little time, was the only one in the whole room not smoking. This surprised her because some of the girls she knew to be from homes of Latter-day Saint affiliation, some active ones. She felt a little out of place, wondered whether it wouldn't be appropriate to just hold a cigarette though she never had.

But she put that away and was uncomfortable and yet able to associate to an extent, when the next step occurred. A sixteen-year-old girl broke out a case of champagne her dad had been thoughtful enough to provide, and they all began to drink it. Pretty soon, Gerry discovered that almost literally she was on one side of the room and they on the other. I don't want to suggest she felt very good about it, or noble, or heroic, or like Joan of Arc; she felt terrible. She was under a kind of pressure and with influences she was not used to. She wanted to succeed; she didn't want to be, right in the beginning, characterized as one who was foolish or prudish or ridiculous. She stood and thought, considered holding a glass—this wouldn't hurt—then decided she couldn't do that. And almost literally, I repeat, found herself isolated from them to the point that finally, in accompaniment to their jeers and sneers and laughter, she left the place, walked all the way down the canyon, got home sobbing and disconsolate, heartbroken.

Her mother talked to her for a time and then invited me to. I told her the story of Lehi's vision; do you remember it? Just a point or two. Lehi had a vision of a great tree on which was fruit more desirable than any other fruit in the world. You had to get to it by way of a path alongside of which ran a rod of iron. There were mists of darkness coming up to obscure the path from a big chasm running alongside. Across the chasm was a large and spacious building filled with people dressed in the most impressive finery, having a real big time pointing their fingers at and laughing at the people across the chasm who had eaten the fruit and knew the value of it, it being the tree of the love of God or the tree of life. Well, I talked to her a little, told her I was not a prophet and didn't pretend to be, but that I would be willing, knowing that life is made of not one decision but a lot of them, yet to tell her that in my opinion the decision she had just made was an heroic and a great one, and that the day would come when, with a husband worthy of her and children whom she loved as she then could not understand she would love them, she would kneel down and thank God for the decisions of that hour. Well, that day came.

(*BYU Speeches of the Year,* "Heroism," 1958-59.)

# MARION D. HANKS

## *"Happiest Birthday"*

I mention service and give you one example. I do not think you can really be happy without service (and there is not a whole lot of competition in some of these things!). Here is rather an unusual example: Our daughter's ten-year-old birth anniversary came in August. This is a little girl who is sensitive to spiritual things. She has learned one thing at least that is good from her father. When I have a birthday, I do not think I deserve anything, but I remember the people who had something to do with making my life possible and meaningful. This is the day my mother ought to be honored, not I. Nancy has acquired that viewpoint. For weeks before her birthday she showed, for us, unusual interest in its coming, because she is usually very calm on the surface and does not seem to get excited. When birthday morning came she was in the big bedroom early, with all the family. She had, with her own hands and mind, fashioned something for every member of the family for her birthday. She was not much concerned with what she got. Her own presents were anticlimactical. She did not seem very much interested in them. But there was joy on her face when she gave Dad and Mom what she had made and written. The most precious gift she could have given me is the little poem she wrote about her father. She gave something to each other child, including her little baby brother. I want to share this with you as a simple little example, maybe a little unusual, but . . . as fine a recent example as I have seen. If you want to be happy, *serve*. This was her happiest birthday. She will have lots of other happy ones if she keeps this same attitude. Of course, I am not really talking about birthdays, but of principle.

(BYU Religious Life Series No. 7, "How To Be Happy," 1963 p. 8.)

## MARION D. HANKS

### *"I'm Too Busy Building Fires"*

It was on such a frosty morning as this, as I heard the story, that a railroad tycoon became lost in the mountains, and only by great good fortune was he able to find his way out of the hills. He discovered (of all things) a rail line that led him (of all places) to a small shack which turned out to be an outpost of his own railroad. Filled with joy at the great reprieve of life he had received, he went into the shack suffused with good will, only to have his newly won appreciation turn into distress because it was as cold inside as out. Only in a sequestered corner was it warm; and in that corner a man sat, the one-man operator of this outpost station, tapping out telegrams on the key.

The tycoon became annoyed at the fact that it was warm only in this little secluded area to which he had no access, and said to the man impatiently, "Why don't you build a fire in this place so people can stay warm?" The man, not knowing whom he was talking to, of course, said, "Look bud, I'm too busy sending wires to build fires." The railroad president took his card, reached for a telegraph blank and wrote a little message, put his card with the blank across the counter, and waited. The railroad telegrapher read the message which was "By return wire, fire this man" and looked at the card, gulped, and disappeared. He came back a few minutes later into the larger area of the room with his arms loaded with kindling and coal. The railroad president said, "Did you send that wire?" He said, "Look, sir, I'm too busy building fires to send wires."

(*BYU Speeches of the Year,* "Was He Relevant?," December 17, 1968, pp. 1-2.)

**MARION  D.  HANKS**

## *"Daddy, I Wish You Could Be with Me"*

I will not forget the night when a fine, mature, successful, affluent man stood in a large congregation and bore his witness. It was a witness that testified to me that the thirty-second chapter of Alma also testifies and what my own experience has testified—that testimony and conviction and assurance and confidence about the truth can come with earnest search and the living of the life at whatever age.

The man told of his little boy who at age eight came to his bedside with a message. The man had been for seventeen years a cynical, critical, quite heartless critic of his wife and children who were members of the Church. His business partner was a Latter-day Saint bishop who found his life somewhat difficult because of this man's attitude. The man went on in his criticism through the years, while his wife, in spite of his problem behavior, dedicated herself and her children to the Church. But the time came when this man, having suffered a broken back in an automobile accident, lay in bed for seventeen months. His little boy came and announced that he was going to be baptized and said, "Daddy, I wish you could be with me." The man, mellowed a little under the circumstances of his recent experience, said, "I wish I could too, son, but you come and tell me about it when you get home."

The little boy came back. He said, "Daddy, I have been wanting to talk to you for a long time, and I'm going to do it now. I have just been baptized into the Church. You are a wonderful daddy, and I love you very much, but this is what I want to say to you: I have only been on this earth eight years, and I have a testimony of the gospel. You've been here forty-five years, and you don't know that it is true yet. And the reason is that you don't really want to. You won't read the books Mother has tried to get you to read; you won't listen to the missionaries or the teachers. You could know, but you just don't want to." The little boy went on his way, and this mature, successful, influential citizen, lay and wept and, according to his own account, acknowledged the charge. When he got on his feet again he continued to do what he had started to do while in bed, to pay the price of learning. He "searched diligently," and stood before us as an active stake missionary with some very successful adventures in service, to testify through tears and great emotion that he did now know the gospel was true.

There are all around us examples of excellence to indicate that going to Sunday School once a week, attending a class in MIA—even going to a religion class at this great institution— that these efforts alone are not adequate. If you would know your Heavenly Father, if you would understand his will for you, you must search diligently on your own and get some personal convictions. I commend that suggestion as being the Lord's direction to every one of us.

As to "praying always," this is a subject of frequent discussion among us. We should pray always, according to divine direction. We should pray over our flocks, our herds, our children, our homes, our books, our examinations, our ball games; over our problems, our joys, our gratitudes, our great experiences. We should be prayerful in attitude and in fact. I believe I have learned how to pray. The prayers that I have learned to offer are not literarily noteworthy, nor greatly involved, nor very long.

---

(*BYU Speeches of the Year*, "Seeking 'Thick' Things," March 26, 1957, pp. 4-5.)

---

Marion D. Hanks

MARION D. HANKS

"To Whoever Finds This"

What shall we give to the children? Pray for a sense of humor. "Laughter leavens life" and brings a sunny spirit.

Pray also to be able to pass on the will to work and the urge for excellence; the capacity for moral indignation and the courage to stand alone; disdain for evil and love of justice; the ability to love without condition or question. Do you know the story of the eight-year-old girl in an orphanage, unattractive, with annoying mannerisms, disliked by the teachers and administrators? One afternoon it was reported that she had broken a rule that would justify her expulsion from the institution. Against regulations she had been seen depositing a note in a branch of a tree overreaching the fence. The note was retrieved. It read: "To whoever finds this: I love you."

(*Conference Report*, October 6, 1968, p. 117.)

MARION D. HANKS

"Wait a Minute"

The other illustration is from one of your stakes. In the early days of my service in the First Council of the Seventy, I observed in the records of a stake to which I was assigned that this stake had a very strong elders quorum. I was anxious to discover why. I asked the stake president in advance if we might hear from the three members of the presidency of that quorum at our Saturday night meeting. This was arranged.

The quorum president who spoke was a professional man who had been very faithful in the Church but whose duties had made it difficult for him to devote time to active leadership, and so he had really never before held an office. Now he had been called to be the president of the elders quorum by a wonderful man who believed in him and in his potential, and he took the assignment. He wanted to succeed in it, so he worked and prepared himself and got some good help and started out. He told us how he had divided the elders quorum area into certain segments. He and a companion had taken one segument, his counselor and a companion another segment, and the other counselor and the secretary, each accompanied by a companion, also took segments of the quorum area.

They had started out with what I understand to be the spirit of home teaching in our time, although they were working under a little different program in their elders leadership. They decided that an occasional visit just wouldn't do the job, because this quorum was quiescent, to say the best. In fact, when the leaders were chosen, there were scarcely any others they could count on. So the president and his counselors, with companions, visited these homes, humbly and earnestly trying to get involved in the lives of the men and their families. At the end of the quarter they shifted areas, so that at the end of the year (they hadn't quite finished the year actually) all of the members of the presidency had become deeply identified with every man in that quorum.

This choice leader bore his testimony of gratitude for the opportunity he had had and sat down in tears. I leaned to the stake president and said, "I understand." He said, "Wait a minute."

The first counselor was a young sales executive who had invested great imagination and creative ability in his leadership. He was charged under the program with the responsibility of the church service of the men, and this meant temporal and religious activity projects. Their temple attendance was high, their quorum attendance uniquely high, their sacrament meeting attendance wonderfully strong. They had projects of all kinds. I remember his mentioning one. They had assigned every man in the rural stake to grow a little porker to sell, but the market went down. He turned around and said to the president with a smile, "I forget how much money we lost on the project, president, but every single man in the quorum responded to the challenge and was involved."

When he sat down, I thought I knew why this quorum was what it was, so I leaned to the president and said, "I understand." He said, "Wait a minute."

We then had called to the pulpit a young farmer, married, with several children. I suppose he didn't have as much formal education as his companions, but he had a kind of Abraham Lincoln honesty about him that communicated quickly, and what he said I don't think I will ever forget.

He said, "When the stake president asked me to be the second counselor in this quorum of elders I said, 'Who are the others?' He said, 'Brother . . . and Brother . . .' And I said, 'I don't know those fellows very well. Do they intend to succeed, or are they going to fail?' The president said, 'We assume they intend to succeed.' 'If they intend to succeed, I will take the job. If they are going to fail I don't want any thing to do with it. I am not about to get associated with an outfit that starts out to fail.'

"Well," he said, "the president asked them and they said they intended to succeed, so I took the job. Now," he said, without the trace of a smile (and I think it was really a guileless statement, although all of us laughed a little), "I want to tell you that these are successful priesthood leaders. They are great, successful priesthood leaders; and the reason they are is me."

Let me quickly tell you again, he wasn't being immodest or arrogant. The people responded. They knew him. They knew he meant it and how he meant it.

---

(*Conference Report*, October 1, 1966, pp. 80-81.)

MARION D. HANKS

## *"Donna"*

In another city, long enough ago that the story can now be told without likelihood of the recognition of the individuals involved, I heard another and different story.

Let's use the name Donna to designate another sweet young lady who left her home for a nearby bigger city for employment. She had a great desire to attend a Church university and needed funds to help her achieve her ambition. She failed to find work in the big city, and as time went by she became more and more discouraged. Then through a series of incidents, she came into the influence of an unscrupulous and designing person who took advantage of Donna's loneliness and youthfulness and the discouragement of her inability to find work and led her into an immoral experience.

The experience was horrifying to Donna, and she returned home with a broken heart to tell her mother, and after a time her bishop, of the tragedy.

There was counsel and compassion, admonition and direction, prayer and blessing. Donna went back home to make her adjustments and to begin to learn the sorrow of remorse of conscience and the blessing of gratitude for the graciousness and goodness and mercy of God. Then one day she had to counsel again with the bishop, to report to him that through this one fragmentary, tragic experience it was now apparent that she was with child. Now a different situation existed, and there was additional counsel and an effort to meet this new situation. There was consideration of the Relief Society Social Service program, which provides for such situations, and other possibilities were considered; but the decision was finally made by Donna that she would remain at home in her small town to wait her time. Some efforts were made at dissuasion in view of the problems this course involved, but Donna decided that, under the special circumstances of her widowed mother's illness and otherwise, she would remain there.

Donna stood up in the next fast and testimony meeting and explained her condition. She acknowledged her fault and asked the forgiveness of her people. She said to them, "I would like to walk the streets of this town knowing that you know and that you have compassion on me and forgive me. But if you cannot forgive me," she said, "please don't blame my mother—the Lord knows she taught me anything but this—and please don't hold it against the baby. It isn't the baby's fault." She bore testimony of appreciation for her bitterly won but dearly treasured personal knowledge of the importance of the saving mission of Jesus Christ. Then she sat down.

The man who told me the story reported the reaction of the congregation to this experience. There were many tearful eyes and many humble hearts. "There were no stone throwers there," he said. "We were full of compassion and love, and I found myself wishing that the bishop would close the meeting and let us leave with this sense of appreciation and concern and gratitude to God."

The bishop did rise, but he didn't close the meeting. Instead he said, "Brothers and Sisters, Donna's story has saddened and touched us all. She has courageously and humbly accepted full responsibility for her sorrowful situation. She has, in effect put a list of sinners on the wall of the chapel with only her name on the list. I cannot in honesty leave it there alone. At least one other name must be written—the name of one who is in part responsible for this misfortune, though he was far away when the incident occurred. The name is a familiar one to you. It is the name of your bishop. You see," he said, "had I fully performed the duties of my calling and accepted the opportunities of my leadership, perhaps I could have prevented this tragedy."

The bishop then told of his conversation with Donna and her mother before her departure for the big city. He said that he had talked with some of his associates. He had talked with his wife, expressing concern for Donna's well-being. He worried about her lack of experience and her loneliness. He had talked, he said, with the Lord about these things also.

"But then," he said, "I did nothing. I didn't write a note to the bishop or to the brethren in Salt Lake City. I didn't pick up the telephone. I didn't drive a few miles to the big city. I just hoped and prayed that Donna would be all right down there all alone. I don't know what I might have done, but I have the feeling that had I been the kind of bishop I might have been, this might have been prevented.

"My brothers and sisters," he said, "I don't know how long I am going to be bishop of this ward. But as long as I am, if there is anything I can do about it, this won't happen again to one of mine."

The bishop sat down in tears. His counselor stood up and said, "I love the bishop. He is one of the best and most conscientious human beings I have ever known. I cannot leave his name there on the list without adding my own. You see, the bishop did talk with his associates. He talked with me about this matter. I think that he thought that because I travel occasionally in my business through the big city, I might find a way to check on Donna. I might have done, but I was hurrying to this meeting or that assignment and I didn't take the time. I too talked with others. I mentioned my concern to my wife. I am almost ashamed to tell you I talked to the Lord and asked him to help Donna. And then I did nothing. I don't know what might have happened had I done what I thought to do, but I have the feeling that I might have prevented this misfortune.

"Brothers and sisters," he said, "I don't know how long I will be serving in this bishopric, but I want to tell you that as long as I am, if there is anything I can do about it, this will not happen again to one of mine."

The president of the YWMIA stood up and told a similar story. The bishop's counselor in charge of this auxiliary organization had talked with her. She had had some moments of thought and concern but had done nothing. She added her name to the list.

The last witness was an older man who stood and added two names to the list—his own and that of his companion ward teacher. He noted that they were assigned to the home in which Donna and her mother lived and that they had failed in some visits and made no effective effort to be the kind of teachers that the revelations of God had contemplated.

"I don't know how long I will be a ward teacher," he said, "but as long as I am, I will not miss another home another month, and I will try to be the kind of teacher that the Lord seemed to have in mind."

The meeting ended, and the wonderful man who shared this great experience with me said, "Brother Hanks, I think we could not have more clearly understood the importance of the offices and officers and organizations in the Church if the Lord himself had come down to teach us. I think that if Paul had come to repeat his instructions to the Corinthians that 'the eye cannot say unto the hand, I have no need of thee: nor again the head to the feet, I have no need of you. Nay . . . the members should have the same care one for another. And whether one member suffer, all the members suffer with it; or one member be honoured, all the members rejoice with it' (1 Cor. 12:21-22, 25-26)—I think we could not have understood the point more clearly."

A number of years ago Brother Joseph Anderson and I had the privilege of driving with President J. Reuben Clark, Jr., to a solemn assembly in St. George. On the way I related to him this story, it having recently happened then. He thought a long time and had a tear in his eye as he said, "Brother Hanks, that is the most significant story I ever heard to illustrate the great importance of filling our individual obligations in the Church. When you have thought about it long enough, pass it on to others."

I have thought about it long and often. I believe it illustrates powerfully and humblingly the purposes of the Lord in establishing his kingdom and permitting us the blessing of individual service therein. I now share it with you and pray God to bless us all to understand its implications and to act on them, in the name of Jesus Christ. Amen.

---

(*Conference Report*, April 10, 1966, pp. 151-53.)

---

## MARION D. HANKS

---

### *"Lord, Help Me Know"*

$\mathbf{A}$ man came to Temple Square one day and stood outside the office door, wanting to come in. I knew as I saw him that he had a desperate need, and I'll confess, to my sorrow, that my first thought was that the need probably was economic. We have many occasions there to be blessed with such opportunities. Well, I looked at him just a little bit suspiciously, and then going to the door, I invited him in and saw immediately in his face that the need he had had little to do with economics. He had a kind of glaze over his eyes that comes with a deep shattering shock.

He was not a member of the Church, married to a fine Primary president. This lady and he were the parents of a beautiful daughter, age eleven. This man's parents lived in the eastern part of the country, and the family had decided in a little council, a sweet and fine thing as he discussed it, that the best Christmas present they could give his parents was to send Daddy to see them, because it had been so long and it being Christmas time, the best gift they could receive was a visit from their only son. So he had, although reluctantly, accepted this commission and had gone to see his parents. While there he had received word from people at home that his wife had been in an automobile accident. The little girl had been killed. Through fire that followed, her body had been destroyed.

This was, of course, a terrible shock to him. He was on his way home, and had several hours layover in Salt Lake, and had come to the Temple Square trying to find peace. He sat across the desk from me, and I tried to teach him. I have seldom been more frustrated because I didn't get by that shock at all. I talked of eternity; I talked of resurrection; I talked of the faith we need, of the strength and sustaining influence of the Lord;

and nothing registered—nothing at all. I began to get desperate. He sat, ill at ease and getting ready to move, and I began to pray. My prayer, and I have repeated it so many times under similar circumstances, was, "Lord, help me now." "Lord, help me now." And for a reason I am sure of, and you will accept I suppose, I opened this book—perhaps I should have done it much sooner without the stimulus of the inspiration, but hadn't— the Book of Alma:

> The Spirit and the body shall be reunited again in its perfect form; both limb and joint shall be restored to its proper frame. . . . (Alma 11:43.)

I turned to Alma 40, and read a little more of the resurrection, that ". . . even a hair of our heads would not be lost; . . ." [See Alma 40:23.] For the first time I saw the break come. I found as we talked that the thing that disturbed him most was that this beautiful little girl—and I have little girls; I know about how a father would feel, at least I think I can imagine—the thing that bothered him most was that he could not even see her again, that the beauty and perfection of her little life was gone, and he had no real hope for anything more. But he sat and listened, and the simple therapy was repeated. We read it as the word of the Lord. He accepted it as such. He sat in one of those little alcoves near the door and read it over and over for a long time. When I took him to the airport, the glaze in his eye was gone. He had wept, perhaps for the first time. He had talked and seemed reachable, and we had discussed the principles I had tried to talk of before.

A few months later I heard his voice at the counter. I hadn't heard a thing from him since our first meeting. He was standing there with two rather rough looking men. They turned out to be his wife's brothers, born in the Church. He had a copy of the Book of Mormon opened to Alma 11 and was reading to them those wonderful words, testifying of their truth, telling them that in his search through the record he had found it to be the word of God. He bought a book for them and sent them home to read, these men who had been born into the faith.

I thought then and have thought since many times of the

statement that one who will not read is no better off than one who cannot.

(*BYU Speeches of the Year*, "Seeking 'Thick' Things," March 26, 1957, pp. 4-5.)

## MARION D. HANKS

### *"Could We Wait Until Monday?"*

I want to repeat a short incident about one of my children, the only boy and the youngest in the family. This has relevance to what I am about to say. Richard is a nice little boy; he is seven and reasonably normal and withal a fine friend and a good little fellow. He and I have had kind of a hard time since we are outnumbered at our house—there are four daughters there, all older than he, and his mother. The girls and he have sometimes, since ours is a relatively normal household, had minor contentions over the television set. Ordinarily, of course, he would lose and became inclined to whimper a bit about it. I have been trying to tell him this isn't what a boy ought to do. He must not hit his sisters, but he doesn't whine and whimper either. He has taken the lesson reasonably well. But the contention crept to the point where I am afraid I will just have to publicly acknowledge a reaction that would never pass in your family living centers.

I said, "Look, you five, if I hear *one more word* I'll chop it up!" Well, do you get the rest of the story? I came home not long after, and I heard a little disturbance downstairs. And then someone, apprised that I had arrived, quieted the others. The noise subsided and then I heard these resolute steps marching up from the downstairs family room to the little office door where I was sitting. My son appeared, resolute, clear of purpose.

"Dad," he said, "where is your ax?"

I said, "It's in the furnace room, Rich."

He said, "Go get it and let's chop it up." I won't repeat the whole conversation, just the headlines from there on.

I said, "Richard, you really mean it?"

He said, "Yes, sir."

I said, "If we do, if we chop this thing up, we are *not* going to get another."

He said, "I don't care. Let's chop it up."

"Well," I said, "it costs a lot of money. You know those ball games and those nice things we like to watch?"

Yes, he knew, but was resolute.

I said, "All right (we went through this awhile), if I said it, I'll do it, and we'll have the greatest ceremony since we buried the frog; but if we do, *if we do*, we will *not* get another. Is that clear?"

"Yes, sir," he said.

"No more ball games, no more movies, no more cartoons."

"Cartoons?" he said. "What is tonight?"

I said, "Friday."

He said, "Is tomorrow Saturday?"

I said, "Yes."

He said, "Could we wait until Monday?"

That is more than a pleasant and true little childish story. It gets pretty interesting when it gets personal, doesn't it? When it begins to mean *me* and *my life, my comfort,* and *my desires,* it gets pretty interesting and quite important.

---

(*BYU Speeches of the Year,* "The Banquet of Consequences," October 3, 1967, pp. 2-4.)

# Biographical Sketch

## ELDER GORDON B. HINCKLEY

Elder Gordon B. Hinckley, a member of the Twelve of The Church of Jesus Christ of Latter-day Saints has devoted a major part of his life to Church services.

In addition to his Church duties, he is active in community and business affairs, being a director of KSL, Inc., which operates television and radio CBS afflliates; director of the Deseret News Publishing Company, owner of the largest evening newspaper and largest commercial printing plant in the Intermountain West; director of Beneficial Life Insurance Company; vice president and director of Recording Arts, Inc.; director of Zion's First National Bank; director of Bonneville International Corporation, and director of Deseret Management Corporation, all of Salt Lake City; director of KIRO television and radio, Seattle, Washington; and director of radio stations WNYW and WRFM in New York City.

Elder Hinckley was born June 23, 1910, in Salt Lake City, a son of Bryant S. and Ada Bitner Hinckley. After attending local schools, he graduated from the University of Utah in 1932.

In June, 1933, he was called to serve a two-year Church mission in Great Britain, and in March of 1934 he was assigned to the European Mission with headquarters in London. Within two years after returning to his home in 1935, he was named to the Deseret Sunday School General Board, on which he served for nine years, 1937-46.

For two decades, until he was called as an Assistant to the Council of the Twelve on April 10, 1958, Elder Hinckley was secretary of the Radio Publicity and Mission Literature Committee of the Church, and for the last seven years of that time he also was executive secretary of the General Missionary Committee. He was called to the Council of the Twelve October 5, 1961.

He has filled numerous special assignments from the First Presidency of the Church, four of them being in connection with preparations for the dedication of four temples of the Church: the Swiss Temple, first Mormon temple in Europe, in September, 1955; the Los Angeles Temple in March, 1956; the New Zealand Temple in April, 1958; and the London Temple, September, 1958. He presently is responsible for the work of the Church in South America, including Argentina, Bolivia, Ecuador, Brazil, Chile, Colombia, Paraguay, Peru, Uruguay, and Venezuela.

He is the author of five books, has edited a number of others, and has written numerous Church study manuals, pamphlets, and radio and film scripts. In addition to these varied activities, he served as a member of the presidency of East Mill Creek Stake for ten years, and was stake president for two years just prior to his appointment as a general Church officer.

# GORDON B. HINCKLEY

*"Fear of Ridicule"*

Not long after that I talked with another young man also recently returned from the war. He too had walked the jungle patrols, his heart pounding with fear. But reluctantly he admitted that the greatest fear he had was the fear of ridicule.

The men of his company laughed at him, taunted him, plastered him with a nickname that troubled him. They told him they were going to force him to do some of the things they reveled in. Then on one occasion when the going was rough, he faced them and quietly said, "Look, I know you think I'm a square. I don't consider myself any better than any of the rest of you. But I grew up in a different way. I grew up in a religious home and a religious town. I went to church on Sundays. We prayed together as a family. I was taught to stay away from these things. It's just that I believe differently. With me it's a matter of religion, and it's kind of a way of respecting my mother and my dad. All of you together might force me toward a compromising situation, but that wouldn't change me, and you wouldn't feel right after you'd done it."

One by one they turned silently away. But during the next few days each came to ask his pardon, and from his example others gained the strength and the will to change their own lives. He taught the gospel to two of them and brought them into the Church.

(*Conference Report,* October, 1968, p. 57.)

---

## GORDON B. HINCKLEY

### *"He Was Talking About My Boy"*

There came into the office a while ago a man who wanted to take a car to his son in the mission field. He said, "My son is riding a bicycle and I am afraid he is going to get killed. Can I take a car to him?"

I said, "You can if the mission president feels he needs one."

Correspondence went back and forth, and finally approval was given for the young man to have a car. The father came in after he had taken the car and said, "I'm proud of my boy in the field. We had never been very close when he was at home. There had always been something of a gulf between us. I want to tell you what happened.

"I drove a thousand miles to deliver the car to my son. I went to his place of lodging and rang the bell. He came to the door, and said, 'Hello, Dad. Glad to see you. Is that the car? I'm late for a meeting. If you can come around eight o'clock tonight down at such and such an address where we are having a baptismal service, maybe I'll have a few minutes to visit with you.'

"I hadn't seen him for sixteen months and that's the kind of reception I got. I felt like getting in the car and driving back home. But I went out, had some dinner and took a little nap, and thought better of it. I went to the hall where the baptismal service was held. My boy was the supervising elder of the district.

"I arrived late and sat on the back row. They had just finished the baptismal service and were having something of a testimony meeting. A man stood up and said, 'I'm retired. I've made some money. I've traveled around the world. I thought I had seen everything and had everything. Then one day that young man who is sitting here came to my door. Time was heavy on my hands; I let him in; I listened to him. He intrigued me, and I listened again. He has brought something to me more wonderful than all I have ever seen or all I have ever known. And I want to bear testimony to the truth of what he brought, and before you people here, express gratitude to the Lord for having sent him to my door.'

"He was talking about my boy. I am not a sentimental sort of a man, but the tears began to roll off my cheeks. I've come closer to my boy in one day in the mission field than I came in twenty years at home. I have concluded to be a better man myself. I have changed my life so that I may be worthy of my son."

This is the kind of effect that missionaries have on some fathers and mothers.

---

(*BYU Speeches of the Year*, "The Consequences of Conversion," January 28, 1959, pp. 3-4.)

---

## GORDON B. HINCKLEY

---

### *"He Didn't Have Enough Sense to Wear Shoes"*

I was interested in a story which Brother Callis told me just before he died. He said in substance as I remember it:

"When I was president of the Southern States Mission, I had each missionary come into the office before he was released. One day a young man came in and I said, 'What have you accomplished?'

"He said, 'Nothing, and I am going home.'

"What do you mean you have accomplished nothing?

" 'Well,' he said, 'I baptized one man in the backwoods of Tennessee. [I think it was in Tennessee.] He didn't know enough or have enough sense to wear shoes. And that's all I've done. I have wasted my time and my father's money, and I'm going home.' "

Brother Callis said, "I went up into that area six months later to check on that man. The sense of failure with which that boy went home disturbed me, and I decided to check on the man he had baptized. I found he had been ordained a deacon and he had some small assignments in the branch in which he lived. Later he was ordained an elder and was given further responsibilities. He moved off the tenant farm on which he had lived and bought a little piece of ground of his own. Later he was made branch president. He later sold his farm, moved to Idaho and bought a farm there. He reared his family; his sons and daughters went on missions and their sons and daughters. I have just completed a survey which indicates, according to the best information I can find, that over 1100 people have come into the Church as a result of the baptism of that one man by a missionary who thought he had failed."

No one can foretell the consequences of a conversion.

---

(*BYU Speeches of the Year*, "The Consequences of Conversion," January 28, 1959, pp. 4-5.)

# GORDON B. HINCKLEY

## *"A 1916 Model T Ford"*

I looked the other day with wonder and affection on a 1916 Model T Ford. It brought back a thousand memories of my childhood, for this was the first automobile we ever owned in our family. It was a thing of wonder when we were children. You today know little of these cars. They had no battery, and the source of electricity was a magneto. At night the intensity of the light depended on the speed of the motor. If the motor were kept running at high speed, the lights were bright. If the motor slowed down, the lights became a sickly yellow.

It is so with our minds. If we keep them sharpened on good literature and uplifting entertainment, development is inevitable. If we starve them with the drivel of miserable shows, cheap literature, beatnik entertainment, they become poor indeed.

(*BYU Speeches of the Year*, "Caesar, Circus, or Christ?", October 26, 1965, p. 5.)

# GORDON B. HINCKLEY

## *"My Mission Is a Failure"*

We had a boy in one of the missions who was sent home sick. He said to me, "My mission is a failure."

I said, "How do you know?"

He said, "Well, I have come home sick."

I said, "Let's get you on your feet. Maybe you can try again."

He went to the doctor, and the doctor treated him for about three months. He was a dismal prospect. But he came in and pleaded to go back into the field. He spent thirteen months wrapping books because he could not stand the rigors of regular missionary work.

I was there when he finally left to go home. We tallied up his achievements. While working in the office and teaching the gospel in the evening he had brought into the Church in thirteen months thirty-two converts. "Be not faithless, but believing." Believe in yourselves, in the spirit which God has planted within you as his child, my brothers and sisters.

("And Be Not Faithless But Believing", January 3, 1962, pp. 3-4.)

GORDON B. HINCKLEY

## *"Will He Come Back?"*

SATURDAY, OCTOBER 29: Elder Marion D. Hanks, President Keith E. Garner, and I boarded Cathay Pacific Airways for Saigon. We flew in a great circle that took us over Vietnam and into Pnom-Penh, the capital of Cambodia. From here we flew over the delta country of the Mekong River. It is a beautiful part of the earth, rich and fruitful—and terribly dangerous for those who would seek to rid it of the Viet Cong who rule it.

We were met at Tan San Nhut Airport by Major Allen C.

Rozsa and his associates. He is president of the South Vietnam Zone of the Southern Far East Mission. Without leaving the front door of the airport, we were asked to sign a waiver releasing the government from all liability for our safety and welfare. We then boarded an old C-47, a "Gooney Bird," furnished by the Air Force. The sergeant in the cabin didn't bother to close the door; it was too hot. He said we needed the breeze. The plane climbed into the sky and we were off for a 3½ hour ride to DaNang.

Some wag had painted on the rest room door at the rear, "The Guts Airline. God will understand the true situation." Camouflage coveralls and survival gear hung on a rack in the rear. We wouldn't have known how to use them had we been asked to. We were flying over Viet Cong territory. That seemed all right until the port motor began to lag and cough, and the propeller was feathered. Strange thoughts fill your mind under such circumstances. Our spirits lifted when the motor caught hold again.

C-rations afforded a good lunch as we flew over the towns and villages of South Vietnam, little pockets held by the Americans and Vietnamese amid the vast dark jungle controlled by the Cong.

As we approached DaNang, Major Rozsa said, "If we're going to get shot, this is where it will happen, as we come in for a landing." We made it all right, but as we were climbing out of the plane, an admiral landed in a similar aircraft. He had five helicopters flying shotgun about him, with marines fingering machine guns.

We were driven to the Marine base chapel where we met with our brethren. I shall never forget that picture or that meeting. What a sight they were! What a wonderful group, these young brethren of ours. We loved them the minute we looked into their eyes. Most of them looked so young. They were dressed in battle fatigues, with mud on their boots. They had come down from the Rock Pile and Marble Mountain along the DMZ, where the fighting has been rough and vicious, and where the smell of cordite and death are in the air. As they entered the chapel, they stacked their M-16 automatic rifles along the two back rows and sat down, many of them with a pistol on the right side and a knife on the left side.

This was district conference in the Northern District of South Vietnam. The program of the services contained the names of three who had been recently killed.

After the meeting we ate from a chow line and then stood about and talked for hours. It was an experience both wonderful and depressing to be so close to these good young men, men who hold and honor the priesthood, men who are valiantly doing their duty as citizens of this country, but who would rather be doing something else. I thought as I talked with them that they ought to be in school, at the BYU or Ricks or at any one of a score of other good institutions, acquiring creative and challenging skills rather than walking fearsome patrols in the dark of the Asian jungle where death comes so quickly and quietly and definitely. These are the kids who ran and laughed and played ball back home, who drove the highways in old jalopies, who danced with lovely girls at the gold and green balls, who administered the sacrament on Sunday. These are boys who come from good homes where the linen is clean and showers are hot, who now sweat night and day in this troubled land, who are shot at and who shoot back, who have seen gaping wounds in a buddy's chest and who have killed those who would have killed them. And I thought of the terrible inequality of sacrifice involved in the cause of human liberty.

There are no hotels in DaNang, where the population is growing as more and more men pour in. We were offered beds in an unfinished hospital, but we could not sleep. Every few minutes an F-4 Phantom jet roared overhead northbound, traveling at supersonic speed. With each one, the thought crossed my mind, "Will he come back?"

(*BYU Speeches of the Year*, "Asian Diary, January 10, 1967, p. 5-7.)

# GORDON B. HINCKLEY

---

## *"Can I Get a Copy of That Book?"*

Let me tell you of a letter which we received a few years ago. A man wrote, saying in substance: "I am in a federal reformatory in Ohio. I recently came across a copy of the Book of Mormon in the prison library. I have read it, and when I read Mormon's lamentation, over his fallen people—'O ye fair ones, how could you have departed from the ways of the Lord! . . . how could ye have rejected that Jesus, who stood with open arms to receive you! Behold, if ye had not done this, ye would not have fallen. . . .' [Mormon 6:17-18.]—when I read this I felt that Mormon was talking to me. Can I get a copy of that book?"

We sent him a copy. He walked in the office some months later, a changed man. I am happy to report that a boy who had stolen gasoline, and then stolen automobiles, and then done other things until finally he was placed in a federal reformatory, was touched by the spirit of this book, and the report today is that he is now a successful man, rehabilitated, earning a living honestly for himself and family in a west coast city.

Such has been the power of this great book in the lives of those who have read it prayerfully.

I give you my testimony that it is true. That I know by the witness of the Holy Ghost. And that knowledge to me is certain.

---

(*Conference Report*, October 11, 1959, pp. 119-20.)

# Biographical Sketch

## ELDER HOWARD W. HUNTER

Elder Howard W. Hunter, a member of the Council of the Twelve Apostles of The Church of Jesus Christ of Latter-day Saints, was a prominent Southern California lawyer and businessman before his call to the apostleship in 1959.

Elder Hunter was born in Boise, Idaho, November 14, 1907, son of John William and Nellie Marie Rasmussen Hunter. He attended the University of Washington before moving to California in 1928. He later returned to school to study law at the Southwestern University in Los Angeles, from which he was graduated with a degree of bachelor of laws, cum laude in 1939, after much personal sacrifice to accomplish this. He became a leading corporation lawyer in the Los Angeles area. He is on the board of directors of a number of large corporations, and has been affiliated with the juvenile department in Los Angeles.

He has served in many Church capacities. For many years he was connected with the scouting program. He has served as a bishop, high councilman, and stake president. He has also been chairman of the Southern California Welfare Region.

Elder Hunter married Clara May Jeffs in 1931. They have two sons. His hobbies include a private library containing many rare books, pamphlets, and family history and genealogy.

# HOWARD W. HUNTER

---

## *"It All Started from a Prayer That Night"*

Several years ago a young man came to my home to be interviewed for a temple recommend. He told me of the lovely girl who had consented to be his bride. I knew his parents were not members of the Church, and this fact led to our conversation. I asked him what had come about in his life to cause him to be interested in the Church and to influence him to accept the gospel and live its precepts. This is the story he told me.

Five years before this night we sat together, a little thing happened in his life—a simple thing, yet so extraordinary that it changed his course. He had been serving in the armed services and had been sent to a university in the East for some specialized training, along with two other young men.

The three of them traveled together on the flight which took them to their destination, and on their arrival they went through the procedure of registration and then were assigned to quarters. They were to room together.

He said that during the time they had traveled neither of these companions smoked, and he did not smoke because of his respect for them.

After the three became acquainted with their new quarters they drew straws for beds and then unpacked their cases. Although they were not well acquainted, they spent the evening chatting about their ambitions and their goals in life.

It was past the hour for a reasonable bedtime, and all evening he had been suppressing the desire for a cigarette. He finally suggested that they go to bed. The other two looked at each other, and then one of them said, "Shall we have prayer together before we go to bed?" Then to the other he added, "Will you speak for us tonight?" The two of them dropped to their knees, just as though they had done this all of their lives.

He said to me, "I was somewhat bewildered, but I followed their pattern and got on my knees." And as he did so, some strange fear came over him. He said to me, "I had never prayed in my life, but as this young man spoke to the Lord some warm feeling came over me—a feeling I had never experienced before."

They were soon on their feet, shook hands, and said good night to each other. In a few minutes they were in bed and the lights were out, but sleep did not come to this young man. Something had happened to him while he was on his knees, and he determined to find out what made these two young men different from other men he had known.

We never fully know how our actions and our conduct affect others. We can only try to understand by our reactions to the conduct of other people. Impropriety, looseness of morals, want of principle, vice, crime, off-colored stories, or evil doing never lift our thoughts or give us a good feeling. On the other hand, it is refreshing and invigorating to be with one who has moral rectitude, integrity, virtue, and is an example for good.

I once read these words:

> Example has more followers than reason. We unconsciously imitate what pleases us, and approximate to the characters we most admire. (Bovee.)

The power of example is demonstrated to us when we see the results of the contagion it creates. Benjamin Franklin said, "None preaches better than the ant, and she says nothing."

These three servicemen went to school the next day and, because of their heavy assignments, spent the evening in quiet study, followed by the chitchat that preceded bedtime. Then it happened again—the same thing that had happened the night before. On this occasion the one who offered the words of thanksgiving and petitioned for the blessings of the Lord was the other of the two.

As the lights went out, one of them said to my friend, "It'll be your turn tomorrow night." For the second night sleep did not come quickly. The thoughts of the words which had been spoken puzzled him for some little time, and he wondered if he would ever be able to express himself on his knees as had been done by the other two.

The next day in the classroom the assignment of that evening kept coming back to his mind. He had the same feeling he had had on many occasions in track meets when he was toeing the line in that tense moment just before the gun that challenged every ounce of strength.

He wondered about this fear that had come over him. In high school he had been a student body officer. For two years he had been a member of the debating team. Public speaking was not new to him, but this was different.

That evening, dinner was over and the three were studying, but it was difficult for him to keep his mind on the subject. He kept thinking of those few moments that would end the day. Then it came. All the courage he had mustered that day seemed to disappear from him and he said to the other two, "I guess I don't have much religion. One of you had better do this."

One of these young men, who had seen the same thing happen so many times during the two years prior to his military service, said to him, "Prayer is just a matter of thanking your Heavenly Father for the blessings you have received and asking him for the blessings you desire. It is just that simple."

With this encouragement he got on his knees and prayed— the first time in his whole life.

For the next few weeks, every third night he took his turn and expressed appreciation for the things that the Lord had given to them and asked for that which they desired.

Then he went with the other two young men to the branch of the Church in the mission where they were attending school.

Finally a period was set aside each night for a little discussion in which they taught him the gospel.

Then came the decision and the day he described as the greatest day of his life. One of these young men baptized him and the other comfirmed him a member of the Church.

They were soon separated after this brief time in school. He finished his military training, filled a mission for two years, and then met this lovely girl who was now to become his companion for eternity.

It all started from a prayer that night. Prayer has changed many lives. It has had an effect on our lives, both yours and mine. Prayer is that which brings us in close communion with God.

---

(*BYU Speeches of the Year*, "Pray Always," October 15, 1963, pp. 2-4.)

# Biographical Sketch

## ELDER JOHN LONGDEN

Elder John Longden, age 70, died August 30, 1969 at his home in Salt Lake City, Utah, after a brief illness.

Elder Longden was a native of Oldham, Lancashire, England. He was born to Thomas J. and Lezzetta Taylor Longden on November 4, 1898. His family came to Salt Lake City in 1909 as converts to the Church, when he was only ten.

He was educated in Salt Lake City schools and attended the University of Utah.

Elder Longden joined Utah Power and Light Company in the sales department following his formal education. He left in 1934 to join Westinghouse Electrical Supply and for ten years was manager of the Salt Lake office. When he was called to be a General Authority, the firm named him special representative because of the press of his Church duties. In 1952 he was named district manager of the National Electric Products Corporation, a manufacturing and distributing firm.

His whole life had been devoted to the Church and to the work. He had been an Assistant to the Council of the Twelve since 1951, and was sustained at the semi-annual General

Conference in October of that year. His other Church positions have included services as a missionary in the Central States, assistant superintendent of the YMMIA in the Salt Lake Stake, bishop, high council member, assistant servicemen's coordinator for the Church, and General Church Welfare Committee member.

He was a vice president of the Salt Lake Rotary Club; president of the Bonneville Knife and Fork Club, and a member of the Salt Lake Country Club and Alta Club. He served a term as president of the Intermountain Electrical Association and was a director of the Salt Lake Red Cross and a vice president of the Community Chest. He had also been a member of the Salt Lake City Chamber of Commerce for many years.

He was well known for his beautiful singing voice and gave freely of his talent at Church services, funerals and other gatherings.

He married LaRue Carr in 1924 in the Salt Lake Temple. The couple had three daughters.

# JOHN LONGDEN

## "I Tried to Speak English, and I Could Not"

I should like to give you in conclusion an experience that came to my attention two days after the passing of that great prophet of God, Elder Matthew Cowley. It was given to me by a man who some thirty-five or forty years before had been district president of Brother Cowley down in New Zealand as he labored with those Maori people. He had only been out for two and one half months, and a district missionary conference was called. In one of those sessions, the morning session, Brother Cowley had an opportunity to speak. As the story has been related to me, he spoke for fifteen or twenty minutes in a fluent Maori tongue, so much so that it amazed the older Maori people in the congregation.

After the meeting, the district president and Brother Cowley were walking to a Maori home to partake of food between the sessions, and the district president said, "How did you do it?" Brother Cowley asked, "Do what?" "How did you master this Maori language in such a short time?" A young missionary, seventeen years of age!

Brother Cowley said, "When I came here I did not know one word of Maori, but I decided I was going to learn twenty new words each day, and I did. But when I came to put them together, I was not successful." By this time they were passing a cornfield, and Brother Cowley said, "You see that cornfield? I went out there, and I talked to the Lord; but before that, I fasted. And that night I tried again, but the words just didn't seem to gel. So the next day I fasted again, and I went out into the cornfield, and I talked to the Lord. I told the Lord that I believed his Church and kingdom had been established upon the earth; that men had the authority to proclaim the fulness of the gospel of Jesus Christ which pertained to the salvation and exaltation of our Heavenly Father's children. I told him that I had been called by this same authority to fill a mission, but if this was not the mission in which I was to serve, to please make it known because I wanted to serve where I could accomplish the greatest amount of good."

That was the spirit of Brother Cowley. He said, "The next morning, as we knelt in family prayer in that Maori home, I was called upon by the head of the household to be mouth. I tried to speak in English, and I could not. When I tried in Maori, the words just flowed forth, and I knew that God had answered my prayer and this was where I should serve." A young lad seventeen years of age!

(*Conference Report*, April 4, 1955, p. 59.)

# JOHN LONGDEN

## *"Clarence Romeral, a Mormon Boy"*

Some time ago, I heard the story of a young man who had an inventive mind. He had graduated from college and desired to get into the laboratory of one of the big companies in the United States which spend millions of dollars in research as our good friend here, Brother Harvey Fletcher, can confirm. This young man saw an advertisement in the newspaper and applied. He was one of twenty-seven. On the application blank it asked, "To which church do you belong?" That is quite a serious question. He thought to himself: "If I put down The Church of Jesus Christ of Latter-day Saints, they probably won't know which church it is. If I put down the Mormon Church, that will remove all doubt and probably the chances of getting this position will go out the window." Satan's whisperings. The young man thought: "What should I do?" So he did the intelligent thing. He deliberated. He prayed to God through Jesus Christ, for he knew that that channel of communication was open. He allowed the power of good to influence him and wrote on that application blank, "Church of Jesus Christ of Latter-day Saints," and in parenthesis so he would not be misunderstood, "commonly called the Mormon Church." He succumbed to the whisperings of the still small voice. He was the first one of twenty-seven applying for the position to be called in by the personnel manager. As he sat across the desk from the personnel manager, this gentleman said that he knew something about our Church and that is why he was called in. Some skeptics may say, "Oh well, that is 'happenstance,' it would have happened anyway." But you could not make this young man believe that.

The manager said, "I see you are a Mormon."

"Yes, sir, I am."

"Do you pay your tithing?"

"Yes, sir, I do."

"Do you keep the laws of chastity; are you morally clean?"

"Yes, sir, I am."

"Do you keep the Word of Wisdom?"

"Yes, sir, I do."

Isn't that wonderful, marvelous? I do not have to relate what would have happened otherwise—loss of faith in the individual and in the Church. He must have answered the other questions correctly to the satisfaction of the personnel manager because he was given the position. He was hired to work in the laboratories of the great Poloroid Company of the United States. This young Mormon boy is responsible for bringing out a camera that will take a picture and develop that picture within a minute or a few seconds thereof. Today many times a day this camera is demonstrated on television. Clarence Romeral, a Mormon boy, who had defined the two powers, the power of Jesus Christ and the power of Satan, and had taken advantage of the power of Jesus Christ. Today he is still an active Church member.

(*Brigham Young University Miscellaneous Speeches*, "Two Powers," December 10, 1957, p. 6.)

# JOHN LONGDEN

## *"Going to New Zealand"*

I have had many rich experiences in the last few months as I have traveled in the South Pacific. In Suva, Fiji, last December, there was a group of sixty-nine who were returning from the temple at Hamilton, New Zealand— husbands and wives having been sealed for the first time, children having been sealed to them. As I visited with the leader of the group, I learned how they had traveled on boats—not luxury liners. They had sold their possessions in the first place, to raise funds to go down to the temple. They did not have lovely cabins. They had to take their food with them; they did not eat at the tables. Their leader was proud to tell me, "The captain likes our people so well that he gives us the best place on the deck." They had faith, recognizing the commandments of the Lord and applying them in their lives. Then, as we asked them, "What are you going to do? You have given up your work. You have sold your possessions. What are you going to do now when you get back home?" they replied, "The Lord will prepare a way, as we are willing to work. We have accomplished a great mission."

Then I reflect on the city of Perth, Australia, last Christmas Eve. (At 106 degrees, I tell you, it was rather warm.) We went to the railroad station to see another group of twenty-five or thirty, likewise going to New Zealand to perform temple ordinances for their families. I think of one little family—a young husband and wife with five children, sitting there on the hard seats, not cushioned chairs. There they use little old cars such as we discarded fifty years ago in this country (unless you go back into the hinterlands somewhere—I have not seen any for a long while). Then I noticed on the back platform (this little iron railing open, as they used to be here)—hanging there was a canvas bucket. I said, "What is that?" It was called to my attention that that was their culinary water to use on the trip, as, again, they were taking their food with them. They would have to change four different times because there were four states that they had to go through in Australia, and the tracks of the railroads in each state are of different gauge so they would have to change to other trains. Talk about the need of brotherhood! Yes, I witnessed and visualized all this. But I saw reflected from their faces the joy and the satisfaction and the anticipation that they were going to accomplish the commandments of the Lord. Oh, I am so grateful, as I travel around the Church, to see their faith.

---

(*BYU Speeches of the Year*, "The Lord is My Shepherd I Shall Not Want," November 1, 1961, pp. 6-7.

# Biographical Sketch

## ELDER LEGRAND RICHARDS

Elder LeGrand Richards, a member of the Council of the Twelve of The Church of Jesus Christ of Latter-day Saints, has devoted over sixty years of service to the Church in positions of major responsibility, in addition to carrying on a successful real estate business much of that time.

Elder Richards is the third apostle in direct family descent. His father was President George F. Richards of the Council of the Twelve and his grandfather, Franklin D. Richards, was also a member of the Council; and he is a nephew of Willard Richards, pioneer leader, apostle, and counselor to President Brigham Young. His mother was Alice A. Robinson. He was born February 6, 1886, at Farmington, Utah.

His Church service began when he was called as a missionary to the Netherlands from 1905 to 1908. He has filled four missions and presided over two of them. He has served as bishop of three wards, as a member of two high councils, and as president of a stake. He served fourteen years as the Presiding Bishop of the Church and has been a member of the Council of the Twelve since April, 1952.

In the division of responsibilities among the members of the

Council of the Twelve, Elder Richards directs the missionary programs in the following missions: Western States, Northern Indian, Southwest Indian, Western Canadian, West Central States, and Arizona.

He is the author of three widely-read Church books.

He married Ina Jane Ashton May 19, 1909, in the Salt Lake Temple, and they have four daughters and two sons.

# LEGRAND RICHARDS

## "Thirty-five Million Years from Today"

If you stop to think about it, possibly the most important thing in your life since you became a member of the Church is whom you are going to marry, because you know eternity is a long time and when you marry, if you do what the Lord wants you to, you will remain married forever and that is a long time to just live with one individual. How long it is I am not going to attempt to tell you; but I used this little illustration with my wife when we had been married 35 years. I said, "Mother, what do you think we will be doing thirty-five million years from today?"

She said, "Where did you get that crazy idea?"

I said, "Well, you believe in eternal life don't you? In the Book of Mormon we read that time is measured only to man; that with God there is not such a thing as time. It is one eternal round, and the Prophet Joseph illustrated it by taking a ring. He said, 'When you cut it it has a beginning and it has an end; but as long as you do not cut it there is no beginning and there is no end." I said, "Mother, if you believe that, you and I ought to be pretty well acquainted with each other in thirty-five million years from today."

When you see her walking along the street, ask yourself the question "Would I want to live with her thirty-five million years?"

(Address to the Delta Phi Fraternity Date Night, March 3, 1954, p. 3., Brigham Young University.)

## LEGRAND RICHARDS

### *"I Laid My Bible on the Table"*

We didn't get our Church by a study of the Bible; we got it through the revelations of God the Eternal Father and the sending to this earth of heavenly messengers that have brought back the power to officiate in the name of the Lord and have given us a clear, comprehensive understanding of the truths of the gospel.

When I was in Holland on a mission, I was invited at one time to talk to a group of businessmen—a Bible class. We met in the home of a prominent furniture dealer. They gave me an hour and a half and a subject to discuss. At the close of the hour and a half I don't think there had been one question asked. I laid my Bible on the table and folded my arms and waited for a comment. The first comment came from a daughter of the man of the house. She was the only woman in the room at that time with about twenty businessmen, each with his Bible. She said, "Father, I just can't understand it. I have never attended one of these Bible classes in my life that you haven't had the last word to say on everything, and tonight you haven't said a word."

He shook his head and said, "There isn't anything to say. This man has been teaching us things we have never heard of,

and he has been teaching them to us out of our own Bibles."
Now, that's why we have to have modern revelation. No one but
God the Eternal Father could give us the truth.

(*Conference Report*, April, 1965, p. 117.)

## LEGRAND RICHARDS

### *"A Little for Good Measure"*

I don't suppose I would be standing
here tonight were it not for the noble teachings and example of
that father of mine. I grew up on a farm. When everything went
dead wrong, as it did at times, I remember a hayrack we were
trying to get the gears on; it tumbled down, and the worst swear
word I ever heard my father use in all the years on that farm
was "oh, fiddlesticks!" And I think the Lord will forgive him
for that.

I can remember hoeing weeds out of the old corn patch—
acres of it—when father would take rows and we would take
rows, and he would keep calling to us and asking us Church
questions: "What is the gospel?" I can remember that question
when I was just a little fellow, my daddy asking it as we were
hoeing the corn. You can't get away from things like that.

At the end of the year, he would gather us three boys
around the table in the dining room. We each had a notebook,
and we would figure out the tithing. You know, on the farm it
isn't like getting a monthly check. We figured what the chickens
had produced, and what the garden had produced; and if a
calf was a year older than at the beginning of the year, than we
would figure its growth and the added value. And then after we

had gotten everything all figured out, Father would always throw in a little for good measure, so that we would be sure that we had paid a full tithing.

Do you suppose that any one of those three boys who sat around that table year after year with that kind of leadership would have ever ended a year without being a full tithe payer? Well, you know where I am. I am the middle one of the three; both of the others have been mission presidents; they are both patriarchs today. I tell you, there is no substitute for what you get from a father who sets the example. You know the little story that "he stepped in his father's footsteps all the way."

(*Conference Report*, September 30, 1967, pp. 110-11.)

## LEGRAND RICHARDS

### *"The Lord's Blueprint"*

By appointment from the First Presidency and at their request, I was privileged to meet with a group of ministers here in Salt Lake City who were holding a convention. They gave me two hours and a half to explain Mormonism to them.

I explained the great organization of the Church and how it came into existence and bore my testimony of its divinity. I thought of the Apostle Paul—if he had the scriptures, and was with us today, and had to convince publicly the people out of the scriptures—how much more he would have to explain to them pertaining to this latter-day gospel dispensation and the second coming of the Redeemer of the world than he had in his day.

I used this illustration with these ministers. I told them

that when we built the Los Angeles Temple I was still the Presiding Bishop, and we took the plans and showed them to the First Presidency one day. And we had eighty-five pages about four feet long and two-and-a-half feet wide, and we did not have the plans complete for the electrical work or the plumbing, and yet there were eighty-five pages. Now I said to these men, "You could take those plans and go all over this world and try to fit them to any other building in the world, and you could not fit them. There is only one building that those plans will fit and that is the Los Angeles Temple." I said, "Of course, you could find heating plants, and light fixtures, and plumbing, and cement in other buildings just as you do in that temple, but you could not find a building that would fit perfectly those plans."

Then I took the Bible and I said, "The Prophet Isaiah tells us that the Lord declared his work from the beginning and he said that the 'grass withereth, the flower fadeth; but the word of our God shall stand for ever.' (Isa. 40:8.) And as I see it, the Bible is the Lord's blueprint of his work from the beginning until the final winding up scene."

Of course, there is not time for me to go into details here today, but I took scripture after scripture that appeared in the Bible, and I said to these men, "Do you know anywhere in all the world where you can find a fulfilment of that promise? Take for instance Peter's statement to those who crucified the Christ that before his coming the heavens were to receive him, until the restitution of all things spoken by the mouth of all his holy prophets since the world began. (See Acts 3:19-21.) Do any of you know anywhere in this world, in the history of the world or the history of the people or churches, where that promise has had its fulfilment? And yet people look for his coming." But if Peter was a prophet of God, Christ cannot come until there is a restitution, and I had explained already to them the fulfilment of that promised restitution of all things.

Then I took the coming of the angel that John saw, flying in the midst of heaven. I said, "Do you know anywhere in the world that there is a record of the coming of an angel with the everlasting gospel to be preached in all the world, to every nation, kindred, tongue, and people, since the time that prophet's promise was made?"

Then I went through many other of the passages of scripture pertaining to our day. Like the coming of Elijah the prophet, and so forth, and then I said this to them: "Now, that Bible is just as much the Lord's blueprint of what he intended to do in this world as the blueprint for that temple was the plan by which that building was to be built."

I said, "It is true that you can find some of the things that are in the Bible in the churches, that is why we have hundreds of them, but you cannot find any other church in all the world that has all of the things that the Lord has promised."

(*Conference Report,* April, 1960, pp. 104-105.)

## LEGRAND RICHARDS

### *"I Am Afraid to Go Home"*

When I was president of the Netherlands Mission I went to release one of the missionaries. I always had a little fatherly talk with them before they left. This one missionary said, "President Richards, I am afraid to go home."

I said, "Why are you afraid to go home?"

"Well," he said, "I had companions at home that were not what they should have been, and I am afraid that I might fall back into their company when I get home and drift away from what I have learned here in the mission field."

I said to this young man, "If you will make me a promise, I'll make you a promise. If you will promise me that you will never let a day start that you won't first get down on your knees and pray in the spirit that you have prayed here in the mission field and ask God to preserve you during the day from evil and to prosper you, and you will never let a day close that you do not get down on your knees and thank the Lord for having preserved you that day—you only live one day at a time; like Jesus said, 'Sufficient unto the day is the evil thereof' (Matthew 6:34)—the Lord will give you the strength for each day if you just keep close to him."

He made the promise. I did not see him for several years. (This was during World War I.) I returned home and was in business. My desk was some distance from the front door in my office. One day the front door opened and a young man in uniform walked in with a smile all over his face. I got up and walked toward him, and as we took each other by the hand, he did not say, "How are you, President Richards?" He said, "President Richards, do you remember what you made me promise you before I left the mission field?"

I said, "I certainly do, and you have kept your promise. I can see it all over your face."

He said, "I am just as clean as I was the day I left you."

Now, brothers and sisters, there is help, an unseen power that we can get that will help us; and we need that help.

---

*BYU Speeches of the Year,* "How You Can Best Honor Your Parents," October 29, 1963, p. 7.)

---

## LEGRAND RICHARDS

### "A Chance to Get Even"

Each one of us can wield an influence and touch the lives of others as they come among us. For instance, years ago as I completed a mission back in the Eastern States (I had been released as bishop to go there), one of my counselors came back with his wife and my wife. He bought an automobile (he was in the automobile business) in Detroit, and we traveled through the East. As we drove into the great city of New York—we had a Utah numbered plate on our car—a man honked us off to the side of the road. At first we thought it might be a policeman or somebody wanted to hold us up—until we saw an elderly woman in the car, and then we didn't worry. This man said, "I see you have a Utah license plate."

"Yes, sir."

"Are you from Utah?"

"Yes, sir."

"Do you know where you want to go?"

We said, "We'd like to go to the Roosevelt Hotel."

"Do you know where it is?"

"No, we've never been here."

He said, "You follow me! I was out in Utah a few years ago, and everybody just did everything they could to make me happy out there. I have just been waiting for a chance to get even with them."

We went through that big city all the way up to the Roosevelt Hotel. He waved good-bye, and away he went.

---

(*BYU Speeches of the Year*, "An Uncommon Church and an Uncommon People," July 11, 1967, pp. 10-11.)

---

# ELDER  LEGRAND  RICHARDS

## *"It Is Now 165 Years"*

The Lord said:

> And if it so be that you should labor all your days in crying repentance unto this people, and bring, save it be one soul unto me, how great shall be your joy with him in the kingdom of my Father! (D&C 18:15.)

I had an experience when I was in the South that helped me to realize what I think the Lord meant. I received a letter from a good brother from down in Phoenix, and he was quite an elderly man. He said that his grandfather was one of the first converts out of the state of Mississippi back in 1840. He said, "Since that time my father and his descendants have given over 100 years of missionary service to the Church." There were then 15 in the mission field, and we had three of them in our mission.

I told that story in a missionary meeting after I was appointed Presiding Bishop in 1940—just 100 years after that man joined the Church. This man happened to be in that meeting and I didn't know it. He came up to me after and said, "Brother Richards, it is now one hundred sixty-five years." When you get to adding ten or fifteen years at a time, it doesn't take long to add another one hundred years.

This was my thought: If that missionary who waded through the swamps of Mississippi back in 1840, when they traveled without purse or script—and many of them contacted malaria fever—had only brought that one man into the Church, he might not have thought that he had done much. But in one hundred years there were one hundred sixty-five years of missionary service from that one man and his descendants, without counting all the converts he had made and all the converts they had made.

---

(*BYU Speeches of the Year*, "Be A Missionary," December 7, 1965, pp. 3-4.)

---

## LEGRAND RICHARDS

### *"You Can't Get Away from Love Like That"*

I left home as a young man and came to the city here to board and go to school; and when my father came to town and stayed with me, he would put his arms around me and say, "My boy, I never thought I could trust one of my boys in the big city." (Of course, it wasn't as big then as it is now.) Then he said, "I would trust you anywhere I would go myself." It was just like putting a steel rod up my backbone. How could I let my father down?

One of my boyfriends said, "If I didn't believe there was a God and I didn't believe that some day I would have to answer for what I do here on this earth, I couldn't break the commandments because of the respect I have for my father."

Just another little thing about how Daddy trained us boys. You know, in the country town where I was raised, the greatest sport the boys had was to go buggy-riding in the afternoon on Sunday with their girls. Of course, my brother and I could never go buggy-riding because Father was a member of the stake presidency, and we had to set an example. One day we went to Father, and we said, "Now, man to man, Father, why can't we buggy-ride on Sunday like these other boys?" Father didn't want to deprive us of anything, but he said, "Now, I'll tell you boys what you can do. You can leave one of the best teams home any day of the week you want, and you can quit work at noon and come home and clean up, and then you can go buggy-riding." Wouldn't we have looked pretty buggy-riding around in the middle of the week when no one else was buggy-riding? Can you imagine our asking the girls to go buggy-riding with us under those conditions?

Well, these are just some of the little things that tied us together to that Daddy of ours. I walked into my father's apartment when he was just about ninety (he died just a few months before he would have been 90), and as I opened the door, he stood up and walked toward me and took me in his arms and hugged me and kissed me. He always did that. I received letters from all over the Church when I kissed Father here on the stand once after I became the Presiding Bishop. Taking me in his arms and calling me by my kid name, he said, "Grandy my boy, I love you." You can't get away from love like that, can you?

Now, that is what it takes to make families in which the children will all be married in the temple, and in which they will all serve the Lord. I thank God with all my heart that all of mine are active in the Church and holding positions of responsibility, because Mother and I have tried to set the example. And you have to do it. You can't go golfing on Sunday and then expect your children to go to church and expect to raise them in the Church. You have to go with them. You have to set them the example.

(*Conference Report*, September 30, 1967, pp. 111-12.)

LEGRAND RICHARDS

## *"Our Hearts Have Been Comforted"*

Here a few years ago, seven years ago to be exact, my wife and I laid away in the grave our oldest son, who was nearly sixteen years of age—the greatest sorrow that has ever come into our lives. We had four daughters before he was born. Less than a year prior to that we took him and his younger brother, only sixteen months difference in their ages, into the office of the patriarch of this Church, Brother Hyrum G. Smith, and he gave them each a blessing.

Now I ask you, suppose the patriarch had known that one of these boys was to die within a year, could he not promise him anything? What would it have meant to the eldest son, had he walked out of the Patriarch's office with no promise and no blessing, and the younger son had all the promises and the blessings? For the older boy truly loved God and kept his commandments. When that boy passed away, and I met with my counselors—for I was then president of the Hollywood Stake—I said to them: "There is just one thing. If God could only give us to understand that boy's blessing." I said, "I wish you brethren would help us, if you can, so that Sister Richards and I might be comforted."

A few nights after that I took Sister Richards for a ride. We asked the younger boy if he would like to go with us. He said, "No. I think I will stay home." The next morning was Sunday morning. He came in and crawled up on his mother's bed, holding in his hand the two patriarchal blessings. "Mother, while you were out riding last night I read these blessings." He said, "You see, you haven't understood them."

I think just for the matter of getting it clearly before you I shall read a few words from the two blessings, as they were given by the patriarch. In the oldest boy's blessing, the one who passed away, the patriarch said:

For it will be thy privilege to bear the holy Priesthood and to go even among strangers and in strange lands, in defense of truth and righteousness.

This we could not understand. And to the younger boy he said:

For thou shalt bear the holy Priesthood in defense of righteousness and truth, both at home and abroad.

The boy said: "You see, Mother, I am going to labor at home and abroad, but," he said, "LeGrand was to go to strange lands and strange people;" and he said, "They are not on this earth. We know all the lands of this earth and we know all the people that are here."

And to the oldest boy the Patrarich said: "And in due time thy home shall be a fit abode for the spirits of thy loved ones;" and to the younger boy he said: "Thou shalt enjoy the comforts of a happy home and the blessings of honored fatherhood, for thou shalt see thy posterity grow up around thee, to honor thee in the same kind of way in which thou hast honored thy parents." Now, reverse the blessings and give the younger boy's blessing to the older boy, and there would be no explanation. He said, "Mother, you see, LeGrand's home is to be the home of the spirits of his loved ones, and my home is to be here on this earth, where I will see my children grow up around me."

You cannot tell me that God, the Eternal Father, did not give that fourteen-year-old boy the inspiration and revelation to understand these blessings. And our hearts have been comforted.

---

(*Conference Reports*, October, 1939, p. 24.)

# Biographical Sketch

## BISHOP ROBERT L. SIMPSON

$R$obert L. Simpson, first counselor in the Presiding Bishopric of The Church of Jesus Christ of Latter-day Saints, has had wide experience in business and in Church administration.

A native of Salt Lake City, he spent much of his life in Southern California where he made his home until called to the Presiding Bishopric in October of 1961.

Bishop Simpson was president of the New Zealand Mission (1958-61) where he had served previously as a missionary before World War II. He also has served in a ward bishopric, on a stake high council, as a stake mission president, as a stake YMMIA superintendent, as a seminary instructor, and was the servicemen's coordinator for the Church in North Africa and the Middle East during his military service in 1943-45.

In business, Bishop Simpson was with the Pacific Telephone Company for 20 years, being successively a plant engineer, public relations supervisor, and supervisor of an accounting office when named to the Presiding Bishopric.

Bishop Simpson received his formal schooling in Southern California, graduating from the Santa Monica City College.

During World War II, Bishop Simpson was commissioned in the Air Force while enrolled at Yale University as a member of the Technical Training Command. He served as a captain in Egypt, Turkey, Iran, and Arabia and, during off hours, did special work for the Church with the New Zealand Maori Battalion stationed in Cairo, Egypt.

His special interests include studies of the Maori culture and sports, especially golf. Currently he serves as chairman of the board of five hospitals and is a director of four business corporations.

Bishop Simpson is married to the former Jelaire Chandler of Los Angeles, and they have three children—two boys and a girl.

# ROBERT L. SIMPSON

## *"The Entire Maori Battalion"*

Now I have something very personal to tell you in the time remaining, and I hope that I can do it in just a few minutes. I want to tell you again that the Lord moves in mysterious ways, his wonders to perform. He protects his people and he watches out for them. He is mindful of his own.

As I was being set apart for my mission about twenty-four years ago, Brother Rulon S. Wells, then of the First Council of the Seventy, laid his hands upon my head and said, "I bless you, Brother Simpson, with a knowledge of the language of the people amongst whom you will labor," and I was grateful for this blessing. So I went to New Zealand feeling elated that I was going to learn a foreign language and that this blessing had been given to me, and no one could take it away from me.

But as I got to New Zealand I did not do very much about learning that language. After about three or four weeks had gone by with not much activity on the Maori language, I had a dream. I would like to tell you about this dream. To me it is very real. To me it is one of the significant events of my life. In this dream I had returned home from my mission. I was getting off the boat down in Los Angeles harbor from whence I had left, and there were my bishop, my stake president, my mother and dad, and all of my friends. As I came down the gangplank of the boat they all started talking to me in Maori, every one of them— my mother, my father, my bishop—all talking in Maori, and I could not understand a word they were saying. I was so embarrassed. I was humiliated. I thought to myself, "This is terrible. How am I going to get out of it?" And I started making excuses. Right then I woke up, and I sat straight up in bed, and two thoughts came forcefully to my mind. The first message: "*You* will *have* to do something about learning this language. The Lord has given you a blessing, but, *you* are going to have to do something about it yourself!" Message number two: "You are going to need this language when you get through with your mission." These thoughts kept running through my mind all through that day. Arrangements were made and we had study time alloted each day to learn the Maori language. The Lord blessed me and I was able to bear testimony in the language after a short time.

Then, to make a long story short, the mission was finished, I came home and came into Los Angeles harbor. They were all there to meet me, but they all spoke English. Not one of them spoke Maori to me.

World War II had broken out. All of the missionaries had been called home. I thought, "Now if I am called into the Army, I am just sure that I will be sent right back down to New Zealand where I can also help President Cowley. Maybe the Lord will send me down there to help him with the mission activity between military assignments."

I went into the Air Force, and sure enough, when it came time for overseas processing, I was sent to San Francisco. All the Pacific processing was done here. I thought to myself, "Here I go right back to New Zealand." However, about two days before the ship was to sail with all of our groups consisting of several hundred men, they took out about five of us—that is all, just five—and sent us all the way back to the East Coast for shipment across the Atlantic. I thought to myself, "Well, I guess I can always preach to the Maori spirits in prison when I get on the other side!"

We joined a convoy and went across the Atlantic Ocean. I saw the Rock of Gibraltar go by, and finally the ship stopped in Egypt. We got off the ship in Egypt and we were taken to our American air base. There was a very small Air Force group in Cairo, Egypt. Of all the Air Force units throughout the world, this was one of the very smallest groups. Well, if you know anything about New Zealand, here is Cairo, Egypt, and here is New Zealand. You cannot get further away from New Zealand than Cairo, Egypt. I thought, "Well, I don't know what the Lord has in mind, but I'll just do the best I can, and I am sure that everything will work out all right."

I want to tell you young people that not more than forty-eight hours had gone by when I found that right there within the very shadows of this American air base was the entire Maori battalion—the entire Maori battalion was stationed there! This was *their* overseas base for processing, for all of their fighting in North Africa and Italy. For nearly two years I had the privilege of being there and meeting each Sunday with these Maori boys, bearing testimony with them in their own tongue, organizing them into small groups as they went up into the front lines in order that they might have their sacrament meetings and do the thing that they needed to do. They needed me. I needed them. I want to tell you that the Lord had a hand in writing military orders because of all of the places in this world that Air Force men were being sent, very few were sent to Cairo, Egypt. Why one of them should be selected who knew a few words of Maori and who had an abiding love for the Maori people only the Lord can answer.

(*BYU Speeches of the Year*, "The Lord Is Mindful of His Own," April 4, 1962, pp. 9-10.)

# ROBERT L. SIMPSON

## *"Chant of the Old Maoris"*

**I** guess I should also tell you that after I had been in New Zealand for just a short time, I went down to a place called Judea, in Tauranga. The mission president said, "I want you to go down there and learn how to speak Maori." He didn't say anything to the branch president, but the branch president had assigned all the Primary children to teach me how to speak Maori. I was helping to build a small chapel. While we were up there hammering nails, these Primary children would sit down on the grass and jabber Maori to me all day. They wouldn't speak any English. They knew how to speak English too—they knew more languages than I did. But, they wouldn't answer me if I spoke to them in English. I had to speak Maori to them. They were forcing me to learn this language, that I might be a more effective missionary.

I remember they taught me a little song. Oh, how grateful I was to them! I thought to myself as I was learning this little ditty, "Here I am, learning the great chants of the old Maoris, passed down through hundreds of years. I have just been in New Zealand a few weeks and already I can sing this old Maori war chant." I didn't know at the time what it meant, but I will never forget it as long as I live.

Imagine my surprise when I found out it was "Hey diddle diddle, the cat and the fiddle, the cow jumped over the moon!" The world is getting pretty small, and I think that is a fairly good indication.

(*BYU Speeches of the Year*, "Do Your Standards Show?", October 19, 1963, pp. 3-4.)

ROBERT L. SIMPSON
_____

## *"The Wyoming Cowboy"*

I am going to conclude by telling you just one more story, quickly, about a young man who was called into the mission field. He felt inadequate for the call—his grammar was poor, he did not know how to talk to people, and he felt that he could not carry out his mission. The reason he had this inferiority complex was because he had to quit school when he was 15 years of age because his father passed away. This boy became the family breadwinner—he had to take over the ranch in Wyoming. The bishop assured him, however, that his place was in the mission field now that he was nineteen.

So into the mission field he traveled, half-way around the world, and there on his very first day he was told that Sister Johnson was having the missionaries for dinner, which was the custom of that mission. On the first day they went to her home and tasted the food of that land and learned something of the customs. Sister Johnson's husband was not a member of the Church. He knew the scriptures very, very well—he knew everything that a Mormon missionary did *not* know on his first day in the mission field. After dinner he would get these missionaries in a corner. He would try to embarrass them, and he found great delight in doing so. More often than not the missionaries went home determined that was not going to happen to them again, so they set their alarm clocks up thirty minutes earlier in order that they might get some extra studying in.

But here comes our young cowboy from Wyoming, feeling inadequate in his calling. Mr. Johnson was in the corner with him after dinner, and the missionary was embarrassed 'til tears came to his eyes. The thought came into his heart, "I will go to my mission president in the morning and tell him that I must be released. I have come into the mission field unprepared." Just then something lifted him right out of his chair, and he stood up to his full six-foot-four-inches of Wyoming cowboy. He reached over and took Mr. Johnson by the shoulders, and he pulled him in real close. He said, "Now, Mr. Johnson, I do not know how to argue these things with you. I do not know how to debate with you. I have not had a lot of schooling, but I know *why* I have to come half-way around the world. If you will just stand here for four or five minutes, I am going to tell you about it." Mr. Johnson had no choice. The young elder from Wyoming then had a captive audience. Then, for the next five or six minutes, this young cowboy from Wyoming told the man the Joseph Smith story—the story that rang true in his heart. He had been taught the story at the knee of his mother. He used to read the story as he rode the range. He loved it and he *knew* that it was true, and so he told it to Mr. Johnson with all of the sincerity of his heart. After five or six minutes had gone by, there were tears in other eyes.

To make a long story short, there was a baptism about four or five weeks later. I think you know who was baptized and who did the baptizing. Mr. Johnson had heard the Joseph Smith story from every missionary who had ever been in his home— some who had been all of the way through college, some who had their gifts developed; but never had he heard it with *the gift of the Spirit of God* like he heard it from the unschooled lips of a cowboy from Wyoming on that wonderful day. He was listening to something beyond the words that were traveling from lip to ear. There was something from the heart of this young missionary into his heart—bearing witness to him, "This young man is telling me the truth. Poorly as he is telling it, poor as his grammar is, I know that it is true because God is revealing it to me." And he joined this great church.

(*BYU Speeches of the Year*, "Gifts of the Spirit," October 18, 1966, pp. 9-11.)

# ROBERT L. SIMPSON

## *"From the Mission Office"*

Someone has properly observed that it doesn't take money to pay tithing—it takes faith.

In this respect, I shall always remember the faith of an old Maori brother in New Zealand. As the missionaries came to his humble little fishing shack located well off the beaten track, he hurried to find an envelope that contained a letter addressed to him and in which he had also stuffed a sizable sum of hard-earned money. He promptly handed the envelope containing the money and letter to the missionaries. This fine brother didn't have the ability to read the letter when it arrived, for it was written in English and his tongue was Maori, but he could read the financial figures contained in it, and he recognized the letter-head as being from the mission office. He thought the mission needed the cash amount mentioned for some special purpose, and he had it all ready for the missionaries. After translating the letter for him, it was now clear that the letter merely confirmed his annual tithing settlement and stated the total amount paid for the previous year. His faith was such that he stood ready to pay the same amount all over again if the Lord's servants needed it for the work.

(*Conference Report*, April 9, 1966, p. 52.)

## R O B E R T   L .   S I M P S O N

### *"Last Testimonies"*

I had a very choice experience over the weekend, for I traveled to a stake conference down in the San Francisco Bay area. There was a wonderful sister there who is a member of the Relief Society General Board, Sister Edith Elliott who is the daughter of President George Albert Smith. Do you know what she told me? She told me that, on the very last day of President Smith's life, the family had gathered around his bedside. He was breathing more deeply, and they were concerned. The doctor stepped aside, letting the family draw close. The eldest son leaned over, and he said, "Father, is there something you'd like to say to the family—something special?"

Then she went on to describe this great prophet, with a smile on his lips saying, "Yes, only this: I know that my Redeemer liveth; I know that my Redeemer liveth." These were possibly the last words spoken by this prophet of the Lord in this mortal existence.

I am reminded of an incident just a few years ago, as my own grandmother lay on her bed just moments before passing. She had been in a coma. Finally she opened her eyes and, taking her daughter by the hand, she said, "They've allowed me to come back for just a moment; I've been on the other side." And then these final words: "I've seen the prophets; they're real. Be true to them."

---

(*BYU Speeches of the Year*, "The Powers and Responsibilities of the Priesthood," March 31, 1964, pp. 7-8.)

# Biographical Sketch

*ELDER ALMA SONNE*

In addition to being an Assistant to the Council of the Twelve of The Church of Jesus Christ of Latter-day Saints, Alma Sonne is a prominent business and civic leader in Utah.

He was born in Logan, Utah, March 5, 1884, to Niels Christain and Eliza Peterson Sonne. He has held various ward and stake positions and responsibilities and from 1910 to 1912 was a missionary in Great Britain. From 1946 to 1950 he presided over the European Mission, with headquarters in London. At the time of his call to his present Church position in 1941, he was president of the Cache Stake (Utah).

Since his graduation from the old Brigham Young College, Logan, in 1904, Elder Sonne has played an important role in the business and agricultural development of Northern Utah. He is president of the First National Bank of Logan, member of the board of trustees of Utah State University, Logan, and a director of the Logan Home Building Society and of the Bear River Mutual Fire Insurance Company.

Elder Sonne is a past president of the Logan Rotary Club and has been vice president and a director of the Logan Chamber of Commerce.

He married Geneva Ballantyne May 16, 1912. They had four sons and a daughter. His wife died in 1941. In 1943 he married Leona Wooley.

# ALMA SONNE

---

## *"Bishop, Let's Ride to the Top of the Mountain"*

Three or four years ago I stood before a large congregation in the little village of Laketown, Utah, on the shores of the great Bear Lake. The occasion was a funeral service for my friend, Hyrum Nebeker, a good citizen and a pioneer of that locality.

His daughter, Phoebe, had called me to advise about his funeral service. She told me that her father had selected some of the songs to be sung during the service. She didn't like them because she thought they were inappropriate. She indicated that they were not quite in harmony with the wishes of the family.

"What were the songs?" I inquired.

She said, "Well, the first song is 'We Thank Thee O God for a Prophet.' "

When he had named the song she had said, "Father, that isn't a funeral hymn. Can't you think of something better? Something more suitable?"

He had said, "Phoebe, this is my funeral, and I am going to have something to say about it."

"All right, Father, we'll put it down."

Then he had hesitated a minute, and he said, "I'm sure you won't like the next one. I am almost afraid to mention it."

"Go ahead, Father."

Then he said, "I want them to sing a cowboy song."

"Which one, Father?"

"Oh, give me a home where the buffalo roam,
Where the deer and the antelope play,
Where seldom is heard a discouraging word,
And the skies are not cloudy all day."

"Oh, Father! You'll have to change your mind about that! I don't think the choir will sing it."

"Well, I don't want the choir to sing it."

"Who will sing it?"

"You know those four young men up there from Bloomington who sing as a quartet? Well," he said, "they promised me a long time ago that they would attend my funeral service and sing that song. It might interest you to know that I have already made arrangements with the bishop. Now, the only reason I am telling you is to remind them. I don't want them to forget it."

I said to Phoebe, "They are good songs. They are appropriate songs all the way through. Why, you know when we sing that old hymn 'We Thank Thee O God for a Prophet' that we are calling attention to something that is very distinctive in our Church. Prophets—we believe in prophets. We believe from them came the light by which our faith has been guided in the past. These men called prophets were great men. They proclaimed their beliefs and admonished their people under the inspiration of the Holy Spirit. And right now, it seems to me that the request for this grand old hymn coming from a pioneer like Hyrum Nebeker is most appropriate. And I think you will find that it will be fully enjoyed."

"But," said Phoebe, "he wants everyone to sing it. He has taken the choir and the audience and requested they sing it together."

I said, "That's all right."

"Then he was very particular to say that he wanted the mourners on the front bench to sing it. 'Now,' he said, 'You can't fool me. I'm eighty-nine. You are not mourning over me. You are sitting there because, perhaps, it is your duty. But I know you don't feel sorry, and I want you to know right now that I have reached the stage in life where I'm finished so far as the earthly cares and responsibilities are concerned, and I want to go. If I should remain I'd be more unhappy than if I went.'"

Well, I waited for two days for the funeral service, and then we gathered up in the little chapel in Laketown. The place was filled. There were fully as many on the outside as on the inside.

Bishop Weston arose, and he said, "It is the wish of Hyrum Nebeker that we all join in singing 'We Thank Thee O God for a Prophet.' That means he would like to have everyone here join in singing—the mourners on the front seats, the choir back of me, and this great audience on the inside and on the outside."

They sang the song. I want to say to you I have never heard that song sung with more feeling and gusto than on that occasion. Everybody sang. I looked down over the audience. I saw six or seven young men in uniform sitting near the back. I turned to my friend, Preston Nibley, who sat next to me, and I said, "Preston, those fellows will never sing 'We Thank Thee O God for a Prophet.'"

He said, "Oh, yes, they will. You know they have flown all the way from the Philippine Islands to be present here at the funeral service of Hyrum Nebeker."

Certainly a wonderful tribute.

Then someone gave a sermon. It was an appropriate sermon. It extolled the character of Hyrum Nebeker. The speaker told what he had done, and that he had been faithful to his trust, that he had been a successful cattleman, that in very deed, he was a cowboy in his own right.

And then came the announcement of the second song. The bishop arose. "The next song will be sung by a quartet from Bloomington, Idaho—four young men about twenty. They were contacted by Brother Nebeker months ago, and they promised to sing his favorite cowboy song."

They sang it, and I am here to say to you it was a proper and fitting tribute to this cowboy who had been brought up on the plains, who knew every foot of the country, who had herded the cattle in the summer and who had rounded them up in winter, and who had taken care of them in all kinds of weather. Hyrum Nebeker was a cowboy, and he did his work well. When all of his brothers left the cold and bleak Bear Lake country, Hyrum Nebeker remained and helped in the colonization of that land. Now, great people have come out of Bear Lake. I am sure in this audience there are many. Some of the great leaders in the state of Utah and Idaho began their lives in and around the Bear Lake.

So the funeral was finished. Hyrum Nebeker had made a great contribution, even to his relatives and friends. And when he left, he also left his testimony. He said that death is not the end. It is only the beginning. And he said if we pass away tomorrow, we will begin where we left off today. Someone speaking quoted his words of admonition to his family, delivered at a great family reunion held up there in the country of Bear Lake.

Then Bishop Weston continued. He said, "In the early spring when the snows were receding from the mountains on the east, Hyrum Nebeker would get on his fine saddle horse. He'd ride down to my home. He'd call at the top of his voice, 'Bishop, let's ride to the top of the mountain.'

" 'When?'

" 'Right now!'

" 'Wait till I get my horse and saddle.' "

And soon they were together, riding up toward the mountain on the east. When they reached the summit of that mountain, Hyrum Nebeker turned his horse around. He took off his hat and he sat gazing over the stretches of prairie land—to the north, to the east, to the west. And then he turned to Bishop Weston and said, "Bishop, I feel singularly close to God when I come up here. I ride up frequently, and whenever I do, I pray. I think about my past, and I think about the future, and I try to make adjustments for everything that is apt to come. What do you say, Bishop, if we have a word of prayer?"

Both men on their horses prayed. They prayed for strength and enlightenment to guide them through their journey of life.

---

(*BYU Speeches of the Year*, "A Funeral and a Mountain Top," November 1, 1966, p. 2-5.)

---

# ALMA SONNE

## *"We Love to Sing"*

During the dark days of World War II I drove my car one day from Salt Lake City to Ogden. As I reached the outskirts of Salt Lake City, I noticed a soldier boy standing at the roadside. I assumed he wanted a ride, although he gave no indication.

I stopped the car and said, "Want a ride?"

He said, "Yes, sir."

"Hop in."

Soon he was sitting at my side. I tried my best to engage him in conversation, but he was very quiet and taciturn. He had little to say. When I asked him a question, the answer was either, "Yes," or "No." Finally, I looked over his shoulder and saw in the lapel of his coat one of those colorful ribbons. I naturally assumed he had been overseas, although he was just a youngster—not very tall, a little fellow.

I asked him, "Been overseas?"

He said, "No, sir."

I expected him to comment, but he said nothing. Then I said, "Why the insignia?"

"Oh," he answered, "I got that for behaving myself—for doing something which ordinarily I did not have to do in the Army."

I waited a minute and asked, "What do you mean, by behaving yourself?"

He said, "Oh, just being decent."

"Do you smoke?"

He said, "No, sir."

"Do you get drunk?"

"No, sir."

"Are you a Mormon?"

"Yes, sir, and I am proud of it."

Well, I felt a little closer to the young man when he said that, so I turned to him and said, "What in the world did you do in the Army which you did not have to do?"

He said, "I led a group in singing."

I looked him over and said, "You don't say!"

"Yes, sir."

"How many?"

"Three hundred."

I turned to him again and asked, "Where do you hold your rehearsals?"

"In a churchhouse, out in Riverside, California."

"What do you sing?"

"Oh," he said, "we have a booklet and we sing every song in it."

"You do?"

"Yes, sir, we do. Every song."

And I said, "Do you ever sing any Mormon songs?"

"Sure."

"Do they all sing them?"

"Every one."

"What Mormon songs do you sing?"

He thought for a minute. He said, "Did you ever hear that Mormon hymn, 'O My Father, Thou That Dwellest'?"

"I've heard it a couple of times."

"We sing that."

"Well," I said, "that's pretty good. Do they all join in singing that great hymn?"

"Oh, yes, they all sing. They love to sing." He was loosened up a bit and began to talk a little more freely. "You know, yesterday when we were meeting out there in Riverside, we were just about to dismiss the boys (as he called them). Just then the commanding officer walked in and stood way down at the back.

"As the boys were about to leave, he shouted to me, 'Do you know that Mormon hymn, "O My Father, Thou That Dwellest"?'

"I answered, 'Yes, we know it.'

" 'Let's have it.'

"We got them all together again and we began to sing. Then the officer walked up to the front, took a position at my side, and put his arm over my shoulder. He reached for the booklet, and as we finished the song he said, 'Wait a minute, men. I want to tell you something. You have just sung one of the greatest hymns in the world. I am going to ask you to do something about it. I want you to know it so well that when you get overseas—which you will—and perhaps on the field of battle, you can sing that song and think about it, because it is one of the finest philosophies in the world.'

"Then he took the booklet and he read from the hymn:

> For a wise and glorious purpose
> Thou hast placed me here on earth,
> And withheld the recollection
> Of my former friends and birth.
> Yet ofttimes a secret something
> Whispered, "You're a stranger here;"
> And I felt that I had wandered
> From a more exalted sphere.

Then the young man turned to me. "You know, he read the last verse too."

> When I leave this frail existence,
> When I lay this mortal by,
> Father, Mother, may I meet you
> In your royal courts on high?
> Then, at length, when I've completed
> All you sent me forth to do,
> With your mutual approbation
> Let me come and dwell with you.

My friends, can you think of a finer message for soldier boys who are on the battlefield and who are facing the issue of life and death? Don't you think that message is most reassuring and comforting? And what do you think of that boy who was leading three hundred men like himself in singing? You know, he is a product of Mormonism. He was letting his light shine before men. He was doing the thing which he wanted to do.

(*BYU Speeches of the Year*, "Let Your Light So Shine," January 24, 1962, pp. 2-5.)

# Biographical Sketch

## PRESIDENT NATHAN ELDON TANNER

President Nathan Eldon Tanner, a former industrial and political leader in West Canada, was named Second Counselor in the First Presidency, The Church of Jesus Christ of Latter-day Saints, October 4, 1963. After the death of President David O. McKay, he was called by President Joseph Fielding Smith to serve in the same capacity in the new First Presidency. He served as a member of the Council of Twelve Apostles for a year, and as an Assistant to the Twelve for two years.

His career in Canada began in the public schools of Alberta. He was principal in Hill Spring from 1919-28 and in Cardston from 1928-32, during which time he also served one term on the town council. Next, he was elected to the Alberta Legislature, becoming speaker of that body. Later, he was appointed Minister of Lands and Mines in the provincial cabinet where he served from 1937-52. He served also as chairman of the Alberta Research Council in 1942 and provincial commissioner of the Boy Scouts Association in 1946.

From 1952 to 1958, he was a leader in Canadian industry, serving first as president of Merrill Petroleums, Ltd., and director of the Toronto Dominion Bank of Canada and of the National Trust Company. He later became president of the Trans-Canada Pipe Line, from which position he retired in 1958. More recently, he was named president of the Canadian Gas Association and a member of the Board of Governors of the University of Alberta.

As a Church worker, President Tanner has filled responsible positions as bishop of the Cardston First Ward and president of the Edmonton Branch. He presided over the Calgary Stake from 1953 until his ordination as a General Authority of the Church in 1960. On April 9, 1961, he was appointed president of the West European Mission, from which he was released in January, 1963. Returning to Salt Lake City, he was appointed president of the Genealogical Society of the Church.

He was ordained an apostle and became a member of the Council of the Twelve in October 1962 and was selected as second counselor to President David O. McKay in October 1963. In January 1970 he was chosen by President Joseph Fielding Smith as second counselor in the First Presidency.

Though his family moved to Alberta, Canada, in 1897, he was born in Salt Lake City, May 9, 1898, and was taken to Canada when three weeks old, where he lived continuously until his call to Salt Lake City.

He married Sara Isabelle Merrill of Hill Spring, Alberta, December 20, 1919. They have five daughters.

He became a citizen of the United States on May 2, 1966.

# N. ELDON TANNER

*"Have a Good Time"*

I have told this little story so many times, but I want to tell it to you today. As President Wilkinson said, we have five daughters. Four of them were courting at one time, or being courted. I do not know which it was. One of those girls had a girl friend in the house this evening and two young men called for them. I sat and talked to them. I just love young people. I *really* love young people. I have great confidence in them. I have great faith in them. I was so happy that while we were raising those five daughters I never lost faith or confidence in those girls. That is the way I feel about the young people today. There are a few who have been hurt—not because they wanted to, but because they had not decided to make up their minds what they wanted to do and set about to discipline themselves to accomplish it. That is all.

Anyway, while we were sitting there talking, and just before they were ready to leave, I said, "Now, have a good time." Then just as they were going out of the door I went over to my daughter and said, "Now, behave yourself."

She said, "Well, Dad, make up your mind."

Then I said, so they could all hear me, "Kids, have a good

time tonight. Have the best time you have ever had. But have the kind of time that tomorrow night, next week, next year, or ten years from now you will still think you had a good time."

That is what I would like to leave for you to think about. Have a good time. That was the slogan we had in the West European Mission: "Have a good time." I would like you all to have a good time.

I said this to a group of missionaries in Germany one day. After the meeting, one of the missionaries came up to me and he said, "President Tanner, I don't think that it is quite fair for you to tell the missionaries to have a good time. You know, the only way they can have a good time is to do their work."

I said, "Well, go have a good time."

(*BYU Speeches of the Year*, "Choose Ye This Day Whom Ye Will Serve," March 27, 1963, pp. 9-10.)

# N. ELDON TANNER

## *"You and the Rest of the World"*

I would like to tell you one or two experiences that I have had in my life. You know, when I was a young man my father pointed his finger at me and said, "Young man, I want you to realize that this world is divided into two great groups—you, and the rest of the world." He was serious about it, and he made me feel serious about it before we had finished talking. He said, "Regardless of what the rest of the world does, it cannot save you; and regardless of what the world does, it cannot destroy you. It is what you do yourself that determines what is going to happen, whether you are going to be loved and respected and happy and successful while you are living here, and whether or not you are going to meet your Heavenly Father the way you would like to meet him."

When I was president of the Edmonton (Alberta, Canada) Branch we had a young man there who was the only member of the Church on his high school basketball team. That young man and I were pretty close friends, though he was only a sixteen-year-old boy. He said to me, "You know, I don't know how I am going to hold up."

I said, "Listen, you have something that these boys don't have. They don't know anything about our Word of Wisdom. They don't know several things that we have in the Church. They don't know that they are spirit children of God. If I were you, I would just tell these boys something about the Word of Wisdom, and how these things may destroy your body, and how detrimental they are to you, and how they will impede your playing, and so on."

You know, he set out to do that, and he became more or less a hero with those boys. Before that year was over, there wasn't a single boy on the team who was using tobacco. Now, how easy it would have been for him to follow those boys and be one of them. You know, it is easy for anybody to be a follower, and he doesn't gain much by doing it, unless he is following the righteous.

It is a little difficult to be a leader, to take your stand. We have an individual responsibility. The world is divided into the two great groups, and remember, you are one of them. The individual is one of them, and his success depends upon his individual stand.

---

(*Conference Report*, October 1968, p. 103.)

N. ELDON TANNER

## "*I Am Going to Report to the Lord Tonight*"

I recall an experience while I was a deacon. I had a sister who had spinal meningitis, and a very severe case of it. We had been taught to pray. I remember so well how my father used to get us together in family prayer and how he would talk to the Lord. He just didn't say a few words and off we would go to the fields. He kneeled down with us and he talked to the Lord as one man would talk to another. He told the Lord about some of our weaknesses and some of our problems where we had failed, and he apologized for us. [He would say:] "Eldon didn't do exactly what he should have done today. We are sorry that he made this mistake. But we feel sure, Heavenly Father, that if you will forgive him, he will determine to do what is right. Let your Spirit be with him and bless him that he can be the kind of boy we would like to have."

My, that was a help! He used to say in the morning, "Let your blessings attend us as we go about our duties that we may do what is right and [we will] return tonight to make a report." I used to think of that: "I am going to report to the Lord tonight." It helped me materially in the kind of life I lived during the day. . . .

I started to tell about my sister who had spinal meningitis, and she was very sick. I remember one night as we (the family) knelt in prayer Father said to me, "My boy, you hold the priesthood now; I wish you would lead in prayer, and remember Lillie." She had been, and was at the time, very, very sick. They didn't know whether she would live or not. I remember as I kneeled down in prayer with the family and was mouth in that prayer the feeling that came to me, and the understanding, that she would be made well. My sister began to get better from that day forward. Today she is the mother of three children and grandmother of five children; she is working and enjoying good health.

(*In His Footsteps Today*, [Salt Lake City: Deseret Sunday School Union, 1969], pp. 82-83.)

---

## N. ELDON TANNER

### *"The Value of a Good Home"*

I well remember when I was a young lad and wanted to go to normal school to learn to be a teacher. Father couldn't really spare me, let alone finance me. But he said, "If you can arrange to borrow the money to go through school, you have my blessing."

I'll never forget going into that bank. I was frightened to death to go in there and speak to the manager of that bank and ask him if I could borrow $400. (That wouldn't get you very far today, would it?) But it gave me enough so that I thought I could get through by working on Saturdays and holidays.

The banker said, "Who are you anyway?"

I said, "I'm Eldon Tanner."

He said, "Are you So-and-So's boy?"

I said, "No, I'm N. W. Tanner's boy."

"N. W. Tanner's boy?"

"Yes."

"When can you pay this money back?"

I said, "I'll pay it back as rapidly as I can out of my first earnings."

He said, "If you are N. W. Tanner's son, I'm prepared to let you have the money." No security other than my father's name! I thought then, "I'm going to keep my name clean so that my credit will be good, and so that my posterity might have the benefit of an unsullied name."

(*My Experience and Observation*, May 17, 1966, pp. 7-8.)

# N. ELDON TANNER

## *"I Can't Think of a Good Reason Why I Should."*

**I**t's good to be here, my brethren, and to partake of the Spirit that has been here with us this evening and to hear the admonition which is good for all of us. All I wish to say on the Word of Wisdom this evening is to tell you an experience which I told you once before. Some years ago in Canada I was driving along and had two young men with me in my car, and a young man thumbed a ride with us. I asked the boys who were with me if we should take him with us, and they said yes. I picked him up, and after we had driven along a little way he said, "Do you mind if I smoke in your car?" I said, "No, not at all if you can give me any good reason why you should smoke." And I said, "I will go farther than that." (I was stake president at this time.) "If you can give me a good reason why you should smoke, I will smoke with you."

Well, my two young friends looked at me and wondered. We drove on for some distance, about twenty minutes, I think, and I turned around and said, "Aren't you going to smoke?" And he said, "No." I said, "Why not?" And he said, "I can't think of a good reason why I should."

I would like that word to go to all of our young men, and

when you can think of a good reason, and only when you can, then begin to smoke.

(*Conference Report,* April 1965, p. 93.)

N. ELDON TANNER

## *"He Had Real Courage"*

Two years after this Church was organized, two missionaries of the Church were out in a rural area where there was a man by the name of John Tanner. That man heard that some missionaries from a new church were going to have a meeting in the schoolhouse. Though he was a cripple, and had been for months, and the doctors couldn't find a cure for his ailment—he was in a wheelchair—he insisted that his boys take him to hear those missionaries speak so that he could put them right—keep them in their place and see that no false doctrine was taught.

He sat right down in front of the speaker, and he heard the one missionary tell about the restoration of the gospel and the apostasy; and the other told about the Book of Mormon, that the priesthood was restored, and so on. John sat there and listened to them, and he never checked them on anything, he didn't heckle them, he didn't try to put them right.

When the meeting was over he said to his son, "I want to meet those missionaries." His son went up and got the missionaries and brought them down and introduced them to him. John said, "Would you men like to come and stay with me tonight in my home?" There he discussed the gospel with them for hours, on into the early hours of the morning. He finally said, "If I weren't a cripple, I think I would like to apply for baptism." See the change in that man that took place in less than twenty-four hours when the gospel was preached to him!

One of the missionaries said, "Do you think the Lord could heal you?"

He thought about it and said, "I think he could if he wanted to."

Then they told him that the Lord has said, "Is any sick among you? let him call for the elders of the church; and let them pray over him. . . ." (James 5:14.) They said, "We are elders and we hold the priesthood of God, which is the power of God delegated to man to act in his name. Would you like us to administer to you?"

He said, "Yes."

They administered to him, and that very day he left his wheel chair and got up and walked three-quarters of a mile to be baptized, and never went back to his wheel chair. He had real courage, and I am so thrilled to think that that great-great-grandfather of mine had the courage to join the Church and to realize that the thing that meant most in his life was the gospel plan of life and salvation. Because he lived up to the teachings of the gospel, and his son, and his son, and his son (who was my father) did the same thing, I am here today. The most important thing in the lives of any one of those men was the gospel of Jesus Christ and living its teachings.

---

(*BYU Speeches of the Year,* "My Experiences and Observations," May 17, 1966, pp. 6-7.)

## N. ELDON TANNER

---

### *"That Is What I Am Saying to You Today, Mr. Armstrong"*

$O$ne other experience that I had has meant a great deal to me, and I think it probably exemplifies what our missionary work is doing throughout the world. I had the privilege of meeting a very fine young man who had been directing plays in the city of London. One of his plays ran for nearly two years. But he had left this play business and had decided to go into the country and live and began to raise race horses. There is a person right here in your state who wanted to buy one of those race horses. He knew me and I knew him well and he asked me to go and see this horse and see if I would pass on it. He chose a poor judge but I accepted the assignment anyway. I had the opportunity of traveling with this man for a period of two and one-half hours. During that time, for some reason or other, we began to talk about the Church. I asked him what he knew about the gospel and he told me. I asked him if he would like to know more and he said, "Yes." And he knew something about it. I told him about Joseph Smith's experience and the Book of Mormon—that it is the record of God's dealings with the ancient people on the American continent—how he obtained that Book of Mormon, and how it was translated.

When we returned home I said, "Would you like to have a copy of 'Joseph Smith's Own Story,' in his own words?"

He said, "I would."

I said, "Would you like to have a copy of the Book of Mormon? I will be happy to give you one if you will read it."

He said, "I'll read it."

A few days later I received a letter from him saying, "I have read the Joseph Smith story. I found it very refreshing and interesting and I believe it. I am now with Mosiah in the Book of Mormon."

I had the opportunity of meeting him later. He lived in an area where we had no missionaries when I first met him. We spent some time with him. My youngest daughter was with me at this time. She was visiting there. I arranged it so that she told him about the gospel. I thought that he would listen to her better than he would to the old man. Getting it from her would probably mean more to him.

Then later Sister Tanner and I invited him and his wife and two children to have dinner with us. They are very fine refined young people. As we finished dinner, we sat and talked about the Church. He and I went into the office to talk for a little while. He said, "You know, because of the things you have taught me, the way you people live, your belief in God, I would like to have my children raised in your church. How is the best way to arrange it?"

I said, "There is only one good way to arrange it, and that is for you to bring them in."

He said, "Mr. Tanner, I am not worthy to come into a church like this. I'm just not worthy."

I had the great opportunity of teaching to him one of the finest principles of our gospel—the principle of repentance.

He said, "You know, this show business is not a good life. I was living an immoral life. I am just not worthy."

I said, "Have you forsaken your ways?"

He said, "I certainly have. I did it before I got married."

"Have you kept clean ever since?"

He said, "I have."

"Do you regret what you did?"

He said, "I do."

I said, "You have confessed. You have forsaken. You are asking forgiveness of the Lord?"

He said, "Yes."

Then I told him how the Lord had said (paraphrasing), "If you will forsake, if you will confess, and if you will keep the commandments, I will forgive and forget."

I told him that the Savior said, when he was hanging on the cross, "Father, forgive them; for they know not what they do." (Luke 23:34.)

And Peter said to those who had consented to the crucifixion of the Savior, "Repent . . . and be converted, that your sins may be blotted out. . . ." (See Acts 3:19.)

"That is what I am saying to you today, Mr. Armstrong."

He leaned over the desk and he said, "Mr. Tanner, do you really believe that the Lord would forgive me for the kind of life I have lived?"

I said, "All I can do is take him at his word. That is what he says; and he did not say anything that he did not mean. He made no promise that he is not prepared to keep." I said, "Would you like to have the missionaries come to your home?"

He said, "I certainly would."

While I was at conference last October I received a wire from the mission president because at that time the mission had opened that area and there were missionaries in that field. I received this wire, saying, "The Armstrongs would like to be baptized; have applied for baptism. They want you to baptize them. Can you do it?"

I accepted the invitation. This baptism took place Sunday, the only time we could get together.

_____

(*BYU Speeches of the Year,* "Choose You This Day Whom Ye Will Serve," March 27, 1963, pp. 4-6.)

_____

## N. ELDON TANNER

_____

### *"Preparing for a Mission"*

At a home evening when we had all the families together, each person had to participate in one way or another. When we came to one of the boys who was seventeen years of age he said, "Grandpa, do you think it would be all right for me to give the first missionary discussion tonight?"

I said, "I think that would be fine."

He said, "Well, I have the material here. I would like this family to be the investigators and I would like to give the first discussion."

Seventeen years of age, and he did it beautifully. Why? Because his family had set out to teach him that he should be prepared to go on a mission. Now there is a great difference in being prepared to go on a mission and being given the idea you should go on a mission. There is some social pressure there when you try to make everyone feel that he should fill a mission because everybody is going on a mission. It is most important that our boys *prepare* to go and fill honorable missions, realizing that they are going out as ambassadors of the Lord, and not just to be like other boys.

(*Conference Report*, October 3, 1964, p. 98.)

# N. ELDON TANNER

## "Why Can't You Pray Where You Are?"

When we were at Waterton Lake just this summer, as Grandpa and Grandma, we had two or three families together. Do you know what the kids wanted to do? They wanted to have family night, and we did. One of the boys who is a deacon was asked to take charge because his father was absent and he was one of the grandchildren who held the priesthood. In the discussion one boy said, "What should you do when you are out with young fellows camping or with a group away from home, fishing, or anything of the kind, and before you go to bed you want to pray?"

Someone suggested, "Well, you might go outside the tent and pray. Or if you're in a home or a building where there is a bathroom, you might go in the bathroom and pray."

Another one said, "Well, couldn't you go to bed and pray?"

One of the girls of the same age spoke up and said, "Why can't you pray where they are?" She said, "I have been out with a group of girls and I have prayed with those girls there. All the girls prayed, at least they did when I was with them. They knelt down and prayed when I did."

I thought that was a very fine answer, and I would like to give my experience in addition to that. I have never found it embarrassing after the first time I knelt down to pray where other men were associated. But I have seen men more than once kneel down when I knelt down; or when I got up I found them kneeling down offering prayer. I am as sure as I am that I stand here that every man, wherever he may be, though he doesn't pray regularly, would if he found himself in great danger or emergency be glad to call upon God. We need not apologize for being one who calls on the Lord regularly and who knows he stands ready to answer our prayers.

(*Conference Report,* October, 1964, pp. 97, 98.)

## N. ELDON TANNER

### *"Safely in West Berlin"*

I should like to share with you an experience I had while in West Berlin which made me even more conscious of the contrast and appreciate more fully what our freedom and free agency mean. I met a young man, a member of the Church, who had his bandaged arm (an arm without a hand) in a sling. Through an interpreter I expressed my concern and sympathy, and this is his story:

While living in East Berlin with his wife and two children, and working in a factory in West Berlin his hand was so badly crushed that it had to be amputated. The shock and loss of blood before reaching the hospital almost cost him his life. While he was in this condition, they sent for his wife and children. At the time they were visiting him there, restrictions were imposed preventing any citizen's leaving East Berlin. This meant that he and his family were safely in West Berlin, where they planned to stay and make their home. He said, "To be out from under that domination and to be here where we can enjoy our freedom and be with the Church makes us feel that the loss of my hand was a blessing in disguise."

---

## N. ELDON TANNER

### "He Was Prepared to Go the Extra Mile"

When I was president of the Trans-Canada Pipelines, we had a messenger boy, but needed a second one. The new boy, a widow's son, was a bright young fellow who was interested in all that was going on and always had his eyes open to see how he could be helpful. He wanted to serve and assist others and learn what he could about the business. He was not trying to be president of the company, but he was trying to be the best messenger boy it was possible to be, and he attended night school to be better educated. Everybody liked him.

He had only been there a few months when one of the supervisors who had observed him wanted him to come with him, so he was advanced to a more responsible position. Before the end of the year, he had had another advancement and will continue to advance because of his attitude. He was prepared to go the extra mile. He was interested in his company and wanted to be of service and was dependable in every way.

The other messenger boy was still there as a messenger boy when I left. Of course, he felt that the company didn't appreciate him and his ability. This type of individual usually complains and asks why he is treated so shabbily and why the management doesn't appreciate him and treat him more fairly.

(Explorer Conference, "Eternal Progress Through My Vocation," August 26, 1963, Brigham Young University.)

## N. ELDON TANNER

### *"I Thought I Could Depend on You"*

Another experience: My father was bishop, as I said before. I remember so well that one day he left my brother and me to do some work. We thought he would be gone for some time doing his Church work, but he returned sooner than we expected. (You know, that happens once in a while!) He found us riding calves. He called us over. I will never forget how he looked at me and said, "My boy, I thought I could depend on you." That was a great lesson, a severe punishment to me. I made up my mind then that he would never have any reason to say that again to me as long as he lived, nor would anybody else, not even the Lord.

(*My Experience and Observation,* May 17, 1966, pp. 7-8.)

# Biographical Sketch

## ELDER A. THEODORE TUTTLE

A devoted teacher and able administrator is Elder Albert Theodore Tuttle, who became a member of The First Council of the Seventy in The Church of Jesus Christ of Latter-day Saints on April 10, 1958. From 1961 to 1965 he was president of the missions in South America with headquarters in Uruguay. Since June, 1968, he has supervised the Intermountain Indian Missions.

Elder Tuttle was born March 2, 1919 in Manti, Utah, a son of Albert Melvin and Clarice M. Beal Tuttle. He was graduated from Manti High School and Snow College. He continued his education at Brigham Young University where he received his bachelor of arts degree in 1943, and in 1949 he was awarded his master of arts degree from Stanford University. He has done further graduate work at the University of Utah.

In school he was a popular and effective leader, serving as president of his seminary class, high school student body president, and Snow College freshman class president. Upon returning from his mission he was affiliated with the Delta Phi returned missionary fraternity and was elected president of the BYU chapter. At BYU he was also a member of Blue Key National Honorary service fraternity and was selected in 1943 as the Outstanding Student in Religion at the University.

His leadership ability has been marked by continuous positions of responsibility in the Church. He fulfilled a mission in the Northern States Mission from 1939 to 1941 and has served as stake Sunday School superintendent of Park Stake, seventies quorum president of East Sharon Stake, and stake mission president of the North Box Elder Stake. He has also worked in the Young Men's Mutual Improvement Association and has taught classes in most of these organizations.

During World War II, Elder Tuttle served two and one-half years as a Marine line officer in the Pacific theater. During his military service he was also group leader for the Latter-day Saint servicemen of the Fifth Marine Division.

For thirteen years he was associated with the seminaries and institutes of religion operated by the Church at high schools and universities in the western states. He was an instructor or principal in seminaries at Menan, Idaho, Brigham City, Kaysville, and Salt Lake City, Utah; and director of the institute of religion at Reno, Nevada. He was appointed a supervisor of the Church-wide seminary and institute program in 1953 and served in this position until his call to the First Council of the Seventy.

He married the former Marne Whitaker on July 26, 1943 in the Manti Temple. They are the parents of seven children.

# A. THEODORE TUTTLE

*"Thank You"*

$M$ay I share with you a personal experience? We had spent nearly four years in South America and returned just in time for our eldest son to enter Brigham Young University. Several months after school had begun we received a call—I think it was a collect call—and the conversation proceeded something like this:

"Hello, Dad?"

"Yes."

"This is David."

"Yes, what do you want now?"

"Oh, nothing."

"Nothing! Well, why did you call then?"

"Oh, I just wanted to tell you about school. I love it. It's great. I am glad to be here. I like the place where I live. I like my roommate. I like my professors and I like the spirit here."

And I said, "Yes, but what do you *need?*"

"I don't need anything."

"Well, why did you call?"

"I just called to say thank you. I am grateful for your helping me to be here."

Well, there was considerable silence on our end of the line and we muttered something about, "We're glad you're happy." Later that night as his mother and I prayed, we thanked the Lord for a thankful son. The lesson, of course, came clear to me. I appreciate a son who says thank you for things that parents have done, as all parents do. But I am a son also. I have a Father in heaven, who, like me, appreciates a son or a daughter who frequently says, "Thank you."

What kind of thanks?

(*BYU Speeches of the Year*, "What Kind of Thanks," November 26, 1968, p. 4.)

## A. THEODORE TUTTLE

### *"Every Time I Open the Closet"*

There sits a young man here today in whose home I was a guest at a stake conference. Since he had recently left for the Y, I was to sleep in his room Saturday night. As his gracious mother showed me the room, she opened his closet where I saw a handwritten letter taped to the rod in the closet. It read:

Mom,

Thanks for all you've done to make this a "special summer." You are a very "special mother" and I thank the Lord for the blessing of being *your* son.

I love you and appreciate all you do in my behalf. See you in November.

Paul.

As she paused while I read it, she said, "Hope you don't mind hanging your clothes out here. This note is still kind of precious. You know, every time I open this closet I read it again, and I would like to leave it there a little longer."

Well, Paul, you are probably leaving for home tomorrow. May I suggest that when you get home you take that sweet little mother of yours in those strong young arms and give her a squeeze so that she'll know you are home—and thankful.

---

(*BYU Speeches of the Year*, "What Kind of Thanks", November 26, 1968, p. 5.)

---

## A. THEODORE TUTTLE

---

### *"He Was Obviously from the Farm"*

There are some four thousand re- turned missionaries sitting here today (and a host of prospective missionaries) who ought to express appreciation to that mother who instilled a missionary spirit in her son when first she held him in her arms, and as she taught and counseled him through the years of his sometimes wavering youth. Most missionaries know that they are to go on missions before they know what a mission is, thanks to the vision and faith of their mothers.

I hope I can always remember the scene that Brother Packer and I saw several years ago. While we were waiting in the Deseret Book Company for some materials, we saw a slender young man, bronzed from exposure to the sun except for the pale border that a recent haircut revealed, purchasing his mis- sionary supplies. He was dressed in a new suit, new shirt, new shoes, and new hat. That he was obviously from the farm was also evident from his parents who accompanied him. His father's rough, gnarled hands spoke eloquently of the years of hard, manual labor. His solicitious mother wore a tidy but faded housedress. His father's old-styled suit, frayed shirt, and run-down heels on his shoes bore mute testimony that sending their son on a mission was not going to be easy. This mother and father hovered around their son suggesting this or that book. Having purchased the standard works and his I.P. book and some miscellaneous things, we heard his father say, "Now, is there anything else you need, son?"

I have thought of that little episode in the lives of those three people—and it could be multiplied hundreds, and I suppose thousands of times—and I have thought, "Yes, there is something more that son needs—a grateful heart and a firm resolve to prove worthy of his heritage!"

I set a missionary apart last Wednesday, and as I handed him his missionary certificate, tears filled his eyes and he said, "Finally! I have waited nineteen years for this. Now, let me at 'em!"

What kind of thanks?

Take a moment for prayer and express gratitude to those who touch your life and make you better. The expression of gratitude is a divine attribute. We need to cultivate it and we need to practice it.

(*BYU Speeches of the Year,* "What Kind of Thanks," November 26, 1968, p. 5.)

## A. THEODORE TUTTLE

### "A Young Boy's Answer"

You have all heard the story of the young boy who fell out of bed. The next morning his grandpa was asking about it and said, "Well, young man, how come you fell out of bed?" And the boy said, "Well, I guess I didn't get in far enough." Now, my personal view is that some men who are on the outside now are there because they weren't "in far enough." Today I am appealing for a dedication to this work that has never been equaled in the past and which we must have if we are to fill that "unprecedented responsibility" that this day demands.

---

(Talk given to Seminary and Institute Personnel, "Men With A Message," 1958.)

---

# A. THEODORE TUTTLE

### *"We Made a Covenant"*

Our obligation as young people is to honor the priesthood and maintain the high standards of the Church.

Our friends can help us do that, and we can help our friends. One of my friends told me his experience. He said: "When I was growing up in our town my friend and I used to hear lots of the boys swearing and taking the name of the Lord in vain. This offended us. Our parents had taught us not to swear. We knew that we should not take the name of the Lord in vain. One day as we were talking about this, my friend and I promised each other—we made a covenant—that we would never take the name of the Lord in vain. During the intervening years, each of us kept the vow which we had made.

"A few years after," he said, "I moved away from our home town to a farm in another valley. It was there that I met head on with trouble. We were hauling hay one hot summer day and had taken a break for lunch. After we unhitched the horses, my father sent me down to the well with a gallon jug to bring back some cool water. I mounted one of our work horses and loped down to the well. After filling the jug I put my finger through the handle, threw the jug over the back of the horse, and tried to jump up on its back. But before I could get completely on the horse, he wheeled around and started off on a trot back to the hayrack, jogging me on his back. There I was, half on and half off, bouncing along on the bony withers of that horse. My finger was so twisted it was about to break with the weight of that jug of water. I tried to jerk on the reins to stop the horse with the other hand, but he would not stop."

Then my friend continues, "With everything going all wrong I got so angry that I swore at the horse and took the name of the Lord in vain. At the very moment I did this, I realized what I had done. A great wave of guilt swept over me because I had broken my covenant with my friend. But worse, I knew that I had offended the Lord, and I had failed to be true to the standard I knew. As I finally managed to fall off the horse, I kneeled immediately—right there in the stubble of the field—and asked the Lord to forgive me. I vowed again, this time with repentant fervor, that I would never again break the pledge which my friend and I had made about swearing."

And he said, "I never have,"

(*Conference Report*, October 1, 1965, pp. 30-31.)

A.  THEODORE  TUTTLE

## *"Let It Fly Clear up to the Sky"*

There will be days when some discipline is needed. Let me tell you a story that illustrates why we put brakes on you, and why we sometimes hold you down. A father was out with his son flying a kite. He had let nearly all of the string out. As the son saw the kite go higher, he said, "Dad, let it go, let it fly clear up to the sky!" This wise father, seeing an opportunity to teach a great lesson, replied, "Oh, no son. If we were to let go of the string the kite would fall down immediately. Son, remember that we have to keep a hold on it to keep it up. Sometimes the things that hold you down are the things that hold you up!"

Now sons, we love you, but we also know you. Ofttimes we know far better than you do when to hold you down, how late you are to stay out, when you are to come in, and when to do many other things. We won't deliberately make any mistakes.

---

(*Conference Report,* April 1967, p. 96.)

# Biographical Sketch

## ELDER S. DILWORTH YOUNG

Elder S. Dilworth Young has been a member of the First Council of the Seventy, The Church of Jesus Christ of Latter-day Saints, since 1945.

Born in Salt Lake City, September 7, 1897, he is a son of Seymour B. and Carlie Louine Young Clawson Young. He was educated in Salt Lake City schools and Weber College, Ogden, Utah.

After serving as an artilleryman in World War I, Elder Young was called to the Central United States as a missionary for his church. Most of his two years service was spent as mission secretary.

From September of 1923 until August of 1945, Elder Young was an executive of the Ogden Area Council, Boy Scouts of America.

From May of 1947 to April of 1951, he served as president of the New England Mission of the Church, in addition to carrying out his duties as a member of the First Council of the Seventy.

Elder Young married Gladys Pratt, May 31, 1923, in the Salt Lake Temple of the Church. She and a son, Dilworth R.

Young, are deceased. Elder Young has one daughter, Leonore (Mrs. Blaine P. Parkinson), of Ogden, Utah.

On January 4, 1965, Elder Young married Miss Huldah Parker.

# S. DILWORTH YOUNG

---

*"An Accounting"*

One time I turned over books to be audited by the auditor for our Boy Scout council. I was keeping the books.

He called me up the next day and said, "Come over. I want to show you something." So I went over. What he showed me was a receipt written in my handwriting for $500 and the bank deposit for that day for $300, also in my handwriting. I was $200 short.

So to make a quite long story shorter, we visited the president of the council. I had said to the auditor, "I can't account for it. I don't remember." It had been a year before and I couldn't remember a thing about it. So when we got to the president of the council, the auditor briefly told him what was wrong, and the president looked at me, and I said, "Sir, I can't account for this. But I know one thing—I didn't take the money. There is an error somewhere and I don't know what the error is. But I suppose you will want my resignation and so I shall write you one. You can do with me what you will—if you want to prosecute me, go ahead. I can't tell you more than that. I don't know."

So I went home and wrote the letter and took it to him. Two days later he had a meeting of the whole finance committee of our executive board, and he surprised me. I sat there and he told them what I had told him. He said, "Dil, we know you didn't take the money. We are instructing our auditor to find out *how* the mistake occurred.

The only way the auditor could figure it out was that I had written a receipt for both the cash we received, which was $300, and the pledges we received, which was $200 perhaps. Nobody knew. I didn't know, and I don't know to this day. I don't know why, but I had a reputation for being honest and truthful and it saved me. I could have been ruined on that occasion and never again would anybody ever have trusted me. But the trust went right on just the same. It never was brought up again.

(*BYU Speeches of the Year*, "Courage to Be Righteous," May 7, 1968, p. 4.)

S.  DILWORTH  YOUNG

## *"I'm Going to Give You a Warning Ticket"*

I had another experience one time. My wife was very ill. I was here in Provo to some Scout affair —I don't recall what it was now—and I had promised her that I would come home by six o'clock that night. I had left food at the side of her bed so that she could have something to eat because she couldn't get off the bed—she wasn't able—and I had to leave her alone.

Things took place here so that I didn't get away from Provo until eleven o'clock that night, and I was worried as I headed for home. The roads in those days weren't like they are today; one went through every town—"Middlesex, village and town," as Longfellow says—and gave the sound of alarm as one went through. I passed through Salt Lake at midnight. Going north on the highway—the moon was full, the light was bright, I could see as easily as in daylight and I was the only person on the road—I went quite rapidly until I got to Farmington Junction, where I was to turn off to go up over the mountain road toward home. I turned off on that road and I really hit it up. I had that car going 70 miles an hour, which was good for those days over that road, and I whipped past the road going over to Hill Field, and down into Weber Canyon. I got about half way down the hill when through the rear view mirror I saw the flashing red light. The patrolman had been hiding up Hill Field road. So I pulled to a stop and got out. (One always wants to get out of his car when a policeman comes, and hold out his hands so he can see that one is not armed—at midnight, anyhow!) It was now nearly one o'clock.

So I walked back a few yards and stood there and his headlights picked me up and he came to a stop about thirty yards away. He got out of his car and came up to me. He said, "May I see your driver's license and your car registration." So I got the car registration and he took a look at it—he didn't bother to look at my license.

I said, "Well, give me the ticket. I've got to get home; my wife is ill and helpless. That's why I was speeding."

He said, "Yes, you were going faster than sixty miles an hour."

And I said, "I was going faster than seventy miles an hour."

He said, "Well, I'm not going to give you a ticket. I'm going to give you a *warning* ticket so you won't do it again, but I'll just warn you. This will make it so you will not have to go to court; but if you do it again, of course, then they'll collect on both counts."

I couldn't imagine why he had given me just a warning ticket. He got the ticket written out and he handed it to me—then he smiled, and he put his hand out, which a cop seldom does, and he said to me, "My name is Bybee. I used to be one of your scouts at Camp Kiesel."

All the rest of the way home, every time the wheels turned, I said to myself, "What if I'd lied to him—what if I'd lied to him—what if I'd lied to him."

I've learned by what little experience I've had with lies that anyone who tells a lie—I can guarantee that that lie will last him all his life and he'll have it burn into his soul over and over again until he dies.

*(BYU Speeches of the Year,* "Courage to Be Righteous," May 7, 1968, pp. 4-6.)

## S. DILWORTH YOUNG

### *"If It Is Told About You"*

*Do not bear false witness.* It's easy to do. We do it all the time on this campus and in other places. We love the juicy morsel about what someone did or what someone thought they did. "If you can't say anything good about a person, don't say anything at all"—you've heard that over and over again.

I don't speak of times when a person is on trial and you are testifying in a court. I speak of the times when you thoughtlessly brand someone with a trait or an act, which may or may not be true, but which you heard. And with a certain amount of pleasure you enjoy repeating the tale to your associates. It is dangerous business.

One time I was conducting a conference in Salt Lake City and President George F. Richards of the Council of the Twelve was there. I invited him to speak and he said, no, he didn't care to speak but to go ahead. So I began to speak, and I told them that if they ever told a story about anybody, that story would stick to that person no matter how long he lived, and it would be believed by most people, and therefore they must not bear false witness.

While I was speaking, I felt a tap on my shoulder, and there stood Brother Richards right behind me, and he said, "I've changed my mind. I want to speak."

He said words about like this: "Once upon a time I was a high council member in a stake, and somebody made a serious accusation against a man. We debated whether to have him in and try him. Finally, the stake president decided he would talk to the man privately, and apparently he did, and the man *proved* to the satisfaction of all of us that not only was he *not* guilty of the accusation, but he hadn't even been in the country when it was supposed to have taken place. He was away somewhere, and he couldn't possibly have done it."

He said, "Forty years went by, and that man's name came up for a very high appointment in the Church." He said, "In spite of myself, I caught myself wondering if the story told about the man was true, even though it had been proven false. I had to get hold of myself to keep from voting negatively against that man on a false story, told forty years before, which was proved false." Then he sat down, and I continued speaking.

That can happen to you. And if some falsehood is told *about* you, you'll know what I mean.

---

(*BYU Speeches of the Year*, "Courage To Be Righteous," May 7, 1968, pp. 6-7.)

# Topical Index

Listed according to author followed by page number.

Abbreviations:

HBB—Hugh B. Brown
VLB—Victor L. Brown
PHD—Paul H. Dunn
ARD—Alvin R. Dyer
MDH—Marion D. Hanks
GBH—Gordon B. Hinckley
HWH—Howard W. Hunter

JL—John Longden
LR—LeGrand Richards
RLS—Robert L. Simpson
AS—Alma Sonne
NET—Nathan Eldon Tanner
ATT—A. Theodore Tuttle
SDY—S. Dilworth Young

## Achievement

VLB - - - - - - - - - - - - - - - - - - 25
PHD - - - - - - - - - - - - - - - - - - 45
GBH - - - - - - - - - - - - - - - - - 134
GBH - - - - - - - - - - - - - - - - - 135

## Brotherly Love

HBB - - - - - - - - - - - - - - - - - - 8
HBB - - - - - - - - - - - - - - - - - - 10
VLB - - - - - - - - - - - - - - - - - - 27
MDH - - - - - - - - - - - - - - - - - 102

## Compassion

VLB - - - - - - - - - - - - - - - - - - 27
MDH - - - - - - - - - - - - - - - - - - 99
MDH - - - - - - - - - - - - - - - - - 103
MDH - - - - - - - - - - - - - - - - - 117
MDH - - - - - - - - - - - - - - - - - 120
MDH - - - - - - - - - - - - - - - - - 124
SDY - - - - - - - - - - - - - - - - - 230

## Conversion

PHD - - - - - - - - - - - - - - - - - - 69
ARD - - - - - - - - - - - - - - - - - - 84
GBH - - - - - - - - - - - - - - - - - 139
HWH - - - - - - - - - - - - - - - - - 143
RLS - - - - - - - - - - - - - - - - - 179
NET - - - - - - - - - - - - - - - - - 205
NET - - - - - - - - - - - - - - - - - 207

## Courage

HBB - - - - - - - - - - - - - - - - - - 10
VLB - - - - - - - - - - - - - - - - - - 25
VLB - - - - - - - - - - - - - - - - - - 27
PHD - - - - - - - - - - - - - - - - - - 39
PHD - - - - - - - - - - - - - - - - - - 50

PHD - - - - - - - - - - - - - - - - - - 68
PHD - - - - - - - - - - - - - - - - - - 69
MDH - - - - - - - - - - - - - - - - - 102
MDH - - - - - - - - - - - - - - - - - 111
GBH - - - - - - - - - - - - - - - - - 131
GBH - - - - - - - - - - - - - - - - - 135
GBH - - - - - - - - - - - - - - - - - 136
JL - - - - - - - - - - - - - - - - - - 152
RLS - - - - - - - - - - - - - - - - - 179
NET - - - - - - - - - - - - - - - - - 205

## Dedication

HBB - - - - - - - - - - - - - - - - - - 12
HBB - - - - - - - - - - - - - - - - - - 16
HBB - - - - - - - - - - - - - - - - - - 19
PHD - - - - - - - - - - - - - - - - - - 41
PHD - - - - - - - - - - - - - - - - - - 48
PHD - - - - - - - - - - - - - - - - - - 57
PHD - - - - - - - - - - - - - - - - - - 59
PHD - - - - - - - - - - - - - - - - - - 63
PHD - - - - - - - - - - - - - - - - - - 64
PHD - - - - - - - - - - - - - - - - - - 68
MDH - - - - - - - - - - - - - - - - - 117
GBH - - - - - - - - - - - - - - - - - 136
JL - - - - - - - - - - - - - - - - - - 154
RLS - - - - - - - - - - - - - - - - - 175
RLS - - - - - - - - - - - - - - - - - 179
RLS - - - - - - - - - - - - - - - - - 181
AS - - - - - - - - - - - - - - - - - - 187
ATT - - - - - - - - - - - - - - - - - 220

## Duty

HBB - - - - - - - - - - - - - - - - - - 16
PHD - - - - - - - - - - - - - - - - - - 64
MDH - - - - - - - - - - - - - - - - - 120
GBH - - - - - - - - - - - - - - - - - 136

## Example

PHD - - - - - - - - - - - - - - - - - - - 41
PHD - - - - - - - - - - - - - - - - - - - 48
PHD - - - - - - - - - - - - - - - - - - - 57
PHD - - - - - - - - - - - - - - - - - - - 63
PHD - - - - - - - - - - - - - - - - - - - 69
ARD - - - - - - - - - - - - - - - - - - - 85
ARD - - - - - - - - - - - - - - - - - - - 86
MDH - - - - - - - - - - - - - - - - - 115
GBH - - - - - - - - - - - - - - - - - - 131
GBH - - - - - - - - - - - - - - - - - - 132
HWH - - - - - - - - - - - - - - - - - 143
JL - - - - - - - - - - - - - - - - - - - 152
LR - - - - - - - - - - - - - - - - - - 161
LR - - - - - - - - - - - - - - - - - - 165
LR - - - - - - - - - - - - - - - - - - 168
AS - - - - - - - - - - - - - - - - - - 191
NET - - - - - - - - - - - - - - - - - - 200
NET - - - - - - - - - - - - - - - - - - 203
NET - - - - - - - - - - - - - - - - - - 204
SDY - - - - - - - - - - - - - - - - - - 227
SDY - - - - - - - - - - - - - - - - - - 228

## Faith

PHD - - - - - - - - - - - - - - - - - - 39
PHD - - - - - - - - - - - - - - - - - - 50
MDH - - - - - - - - - - - - - - - - - 117
JL - - - - - - - - - - - - - - - - - - - 151
JL - - - - - - - - - - - - - - - - - - - 154
RLS - - - - - - - - - - - - - - - - - 179
AS - - - - - - - - - - - - - - - - - - 187

## Gratitude

HBB - - - - - - - - - - - - - - - - - - 12
VLB - - - - - - - - - - - - - - - - - - 27
MDH - - - - - - - - - - - - - - - - - 103
MDH - - - - - - - - - - - - - - - - - 105
MDH - - - - - - - - - - - - - - - - - 113
ATT - - - - - - - - - - - - - - - - - 217
ATT - - - - - - - - - - - - - - - - - 218
ATT - - - - - - - - - - - - - - - - - 219

## Healing of the Sick

HBB - - - - - - - - - - - - - - - - - - 8
PHD - - - - - - - - - - - - - - - - - - 39
NET - - - - - - - - - - - - - - - - - - 202
NET - - - - - - - - - - - - - - - - - - 205

## Inspiration

HBB - - - - - - - - - - - - - - - - - - 4
LR - - - - - - - - - - - - - - - - - - 169
RLS - - - - - - - - - - - - - - - - - 175

## Integrity

VLB - - - - - - - - - - - - - - - - - - 25
PHD - - - - - - - - - - - - - - - - - - 43
PHD - - - - - - - - - - - - - - - - - - 45
MDH - - - - - - - - - - - - - - - - - - 97
MDH - - - - - - - - - - - - - - - - - 117
GBH - - - - - - - - - - - - - - - - - 131
GBH - - - - - - - - - - - - - - - - - 135
JL - - - - - - - - - - - - - - - - - - 152
NET - - - - - - - - - - - - - - - - - 200
NET - - - - - - - - - - - - - - - - - 204
SDY - - - - - - - - - - - - - - - - - 227
SDY - - - - - - - - - - - - - - - - - 228

## Joy

HBB - - - - - - - - - - - - - - - - - - 4
HBB - - - - - - - - - - - - - - - - - - 16
PHD - - - - - - - - - - - - - - - - - - 45
MDH - - - - - - - - - - - - - - - - - 113
NET - - - - - - - - - - - - - - - - - 199

## Love

HBB - - - - - - - - - - - - - - - - - - 19
VLB - - - - - - - - - - - - - - - - - - 27
PHD - - - - - - - - - - - - - - - - - - 35
MDH - - - - - - - - - - - - - - - - - - 97
MDH - - - - - - - - - - - - - - - - - - 99
MDH - - - - - - - - - - - - - - - - - 103
MDH - - - - - - - - - - - - - - - - - 117
MDH - - - - - - - - - - - - - - - - - 120
MDH - - - - - - - - - - - - - - - - - 124
HWH - - - - - - - - - - - - - - - - - 143
LR - - - - - - - - - - - - - - - - - - 168
RLS - - - - - - - - - - - - - - - - - 181
NET - - - - - - - - - - - - - - - - - 207
SDY - - - - - - - - - - - - - - - - - 230

## Love of Children

MDH - - - - - - - - - - - - - - - - - 107
MDH - - - - - - - - - - - - - - - - - 113
MDH - - - - - - - - - - - - - - - - - 126
GBH - - - - - - - - - - - - - - - - - 132
RLS - - - - - - - - - - - - - - - - - 178
NET - - - - - - - - - - - - - - - - - 199
ATT - - - - - - - - - - - - - - - - - 217
ATT - - - - - - - - - - - - - - - - - 218
ATT - - - - - - - - - - - - - - - - - 219

## Love of Parents

MDH - - - - - - - - - - - - - - - - - 105
MDH - - - - - - - - - - - - - - - - - 107
MDH - - - - - - - - - - - - - - - - - 113

MDH - - - - - - - - - - - - - - - - - - 115
LR - - - - - - - - - - - - - - - - - - 168
NET - - - - - - - - - - - - - - - - - 199
ATT - - - - - - - - - - - - - - - - - 217
ATT - - - - - - - - - - - - - - - - - 218
ATT - - - - - - - - - - - - - - - - - 219

## Loyalty

HBB - - - - - - - - - - - - - - - - - - 12
AS - - - - - - - - - - - - - - - - - - 191
SDY - - - - - - - - - - - - - - - - - 227

## Missionary Service

HBB - - - - - - - - - - - - - - - - - - 4
ARD - - - - - - - - - - - - - - - - - 83
ARD - - - - - - - - - - - - - - - - - 84
ARD - - - - - - - - - - - - - - - - - 85
ARD - - - - - - - - - - - - - - - - - 86
ARD - - - - - - - - - - - - - - - - - 90
ARD - - - - - - - - - - - - - - - - - 92
GBH - - - - - - - - - - - - - - - - - 134
GBH - - - - - - - - - - - - - - - - - 135
GBH - - - - - - - - - - - - - - - - - 139
HWH - - - - - - - - - - - - - - - - - 143
JL - - - - - - - - - - - - - - - - - - 151
LR - - - - - - - - - - - - - - - - - - 167
RLS - - - - - - - - - - - - - - - - - 175
RLS - - - - - - - - - - - - - - - - - 178
RLS - - - - - - - - - - - - - - - - - 179
NET - - - - - - - - - - - - - - - - - 205
NET - - - - - - - - - - - - - - - - - 207

## Obedience

HBB - - - - - - - - - - - - - - - - - - 19
MDH - - - - - - - - - - - - - - - - - 111
GBH - - - - - - - - - - - - - - - - - 135
NET - - - - - - - - - - - - - - - - - 199

## Prayer

HBB - - - - - - - - - - - - - - - - - - 3
HBB - - - - - - - - - - - - - - - - - - 4
HBB - - - - - - - - - - - - - - - - - - 12
PHD - - - - - - - - - - - - - - - - - - 39
PHD - - - - - - - - - - - - - - - - - - 64
ARD - - - - - - - - - - - - - - - - - - 92
MDH - - - - - - - - - - - - - - - - - 105
MDH - - - - - - - - - - - - - - - - - 124
HWH - - - - - - - - - - - - - - - - - 143

JL - - - - - - - - - - - - - - - - - - 151
LR - - - - - - - - - - - - - - - - - - 164
AS - - - - - - - - - - - - - - - - - - 187
NET - - - - - - - - - - - - - - - - - 202

## Repentence

MDH - - - - - - - - - - - - - - - - - 115
MDH - - - - - - - - - - - - - - - - - 120
GBH - - - - - - - - - - - - - - - - - 139
HWH - - - - - - - - - - - - - - - - - 143
NET - - - - - - - - - - - - - - - - - 207

## Sacrifice

HBB - - - - - - - - - - - - - - - - - 10
MDH - - - - - - - - - - - - - - - - - 102
MDH - - - - - - - - - - - - - - - - - 117
MDH - - - - - - - - - - - - - - - - - 126
GBH - - - - - - - - - - - - - - - - - 136
JL - - - - - - - - - - - - - - - - - - 154
RLS - - - - - - - - - - - - - - - - - 181

## Service

HBB - - - - - - - - - - - - - - - - - 16
PHD - - - - - - - - - - - - - - - - - 54
PHD - - - - - - - - - - - - - - - - - 59
PHD - - - - - - - - - - - - - - - - - 64
MDH - - - - - - - - - - - - - - - - - 103
ATT - - - - - - - - - - - - - - - - - 220

## Testimony

HBB - - - - - - - - - - - - - - - - - 12
HBB - - - - - - - - - - - - - - - - - 16
VLB - - - - - - - - - - - - - - - - - 27
PHD - - - - - - - - - - - - - - - - - 35
ARD - - - - - - - - - - - - - - - - - 84
ARD - - - - - - - - - - - - - - - - - 85
MDH - - - - - - - - - - - - - - - - - 108
GBH - - - - - - - - - - - - - - - - - 139
RLS - - - - - - - - - - - - - - - - - 175
RLS - - - - - - - - - - - - - - - - - 179
RLS - - - - - - - - - - - - - - - - - 182

## Work

PHD - - - - - - - - - - - - - - - - - 43
PHD - - - - - - - - - - - - - - - - - 54
MDH - - - - - - - - - - - - - - - - - 97
RLS - - - - - - - - - - - - - - - - - 175

# Alphabetical Index

Administration, 73, 110.
Anderson, Jock, 10-12.
Athlete, 72

Blueprint, 164.
Bomb, 102, 103.
Book of Mormon, 139.
Brisse, Lou, 50-52.
Brotherhood, 155.
Buggy riding, 168.

Cigarette, 111.
Conversion, consequences of, 134.
Converts, spreading the gospel, 86.
Cowboy, 180, 190.
Cowley, Matthew, 151-52, 176.
Cullup, Nick, 48-50.
Currant bush, 19-21.

Ebengreuth, Immo Luschin, 92.
Elders quorum, 118.
Eternal life, 159.
Example, 144, 162, 169.

Falsehood, 231.
False witness, 230.
Foxhole, 68.
Funeral, 187.

Gardener, 19-21.
Gem thoughts, 58, 59.
Glove, baseball, 43.
Golden questions, 83.
Gospel, in action, 72.

Happiness, defined, 62, 63.
Home evening, 209.
Home teacher, 64-67.
Hospital, 9, 73.

Iceland, 87-90.
Interviewing, by Pres. McKay, 38.
Irwin, 'Red,' 102-5.
Isso, Sergeant, 70-72.

Jesus Christ, 108-9.
Joseph Smith Story, 180.

Kite, 222.

Lehi's Vision, 112.
Letter, high school, 45.

Mack, Connie, 51, 52.
Maori, 151, 176, 178, 181.
McKay, David O., 18, 35, 37, 87.
Medal, high school, 97, 99.
Messenger boy, 212-13.
Ministers, 162.
Missionaries, effect of, on parents, 133
Missionary service, 167.
Model T Ford, 135.

Nebeker, Hyrum, 187-90.
New Testament, 62.
New Zealand, 151, 175, 178.

Officers, importance of, 123.
"O My Father," 7, 193.
Orphanage, 117.

Patriarch, 169-70.
Patriarchal blessings, 170.
Polacio, Bobby, 16.
Prayer, 144-46; family, 202; 211.
Priesthood man, 63.
Prison, 139.

Radiate, 49,50.
Report card, 98.
Resurrection, 124-25.
Richards, George F., 230.
Ridicule, fear of, 131.
Romeral, Clarence, 152-54.
Rope, climbing, 25.

Scholarship, 72, 76.
Schroeder, Meb, 46-48.
Self-confidence, 54.
Sense of humor, 117.
Sergeant Isso, 70-72.
Service, 113.
Smith, George Albert, 182.
Smith, Joseph Fielding, 54.
Stewart, Charles B., 57-59.
Supermarket, 54.
Swearing, 221-22.

Tanner, John, 205.
Telegrapher, 114.
Television set, 126.
Temple, New Zealand, 154; Los Angeles, 163.
Testimony, of missionaries, 84, 85; 133; of George Albert Smith, 182; last, 182.
Testimony meeting, 15.
Ticket, warning, 229.
Timmins, Barney, 87, 88.
Tithing, 161, 181.
Translator, 93.
Tribute, to the Church, 42.

Vietnam, 136-38.

Warsaw Ghetto, 91.
Wells, Rulon S., 175.
West Berlin, 211-12.
Williams, Ted, 51, 52.
Word of Wisdom, 201, 204.

237